BLOOD ON THE WIND

THE MEMOIRS OF FLYING HORSE MOLLIE A YAMPA UTE

Based Upon the History of Colorado's

Famous Meeker Massacre

A NOVEL

By Lucile Bogue

WESTERN REFLECTIONS

PUBLISHING COMPANY

First Edition

Printed in the United States of America

ISBN 1-890437-50-6

Library of Congress Catalog Number 2001088437

Cover and text design by SJS Design (Susan Smilanic)

Western Reflections Publishing Company
P.O. Box 1647
Montrose, CO 81402-1647

www.westernreflectionspub.com

Dedicated to my beautiful and beloved daughters,
Sharon and Bonnie, and to my niece, Glende

INTRODUCTION

I have lived with Flying Horse Mollie all my life. She is as real to me as my own family, although over a hundred years separate us. I am compelled to tell her story for her before she and I are both lost in the mists of the past and forgotten forever. I must hurry.

Flying Horse Mollie was born and grew up on the White River Ute Agency where the Western Colorado town of Meeker is now located. She starts "telling me" her own story as it really happened, beginning in May 1878, on the Ute Reservation at White River. She is a teenage Yampa Ute, whose band spend their winters on the White River Reservation but their summers up the Yampa River and beyond, in the area of Medicine Springs (Steamboat Springs). There they soak in the hot springs and race their ponies, up on the Flattop Mountains they hunt and gather their winter food, deer and elk and berries and they roam even over into North Park where they hunt the last of the buffalo.

The Utes are the people of the Shining Mountains. Since before the time of Columbus, this has been their land. Always they have lived above the rest of the world, in a heartbreakingly beautiful area of the brilliant blue skies and tremendous towering peaks, of the green valleys and mountains of golden aspens. It is like no other place in the world. Isolated by geography, they are content here in their wild free way of life. They have never had to fight, and so they are friends of the Whites.

Or they have been until recently. A part of their religion is the love of all living things, the worship of Mother Earth and Father Sun, as well as all two-leggeds, all four-leggeds, all winged, and all rooted things. Whenever they hunt to kill, they pray to the hunted, asking forgiveness for taking a life for food.

But by the time Flying Horse Mollie starts telling her story, her world is changing. White men by the hundreds and thousands are crowding

in, threatening to squeeze the Utes off the face of the Earth. It is a terrifying time and a very confusing time for a motherless teenager.

She is often frightened by the life that is so swiftly changing. She begins to question many of the things she has been taught. I love Flying Horse Mollie. She is both timid and courageous. She adores her father, Thunder Cloud, who in return both adores her and spoils her until.... But we will let her tell her own story.

Another reason that I feel so close to Flying Horse Mollie is that she and I grew up as very near neighbors, both in time and space.

First, let me tell you the story of my grandparents, whom I never knew as they were long gone before I arrived. However, their lives lay close to Mollie's. An ambitious young couple from Prince Edward's Island in Canada, they heard rumors of homestead land opening up in the mountains of the new state of Colorado. Even more exciting were the rumors of gold...gold for the finding. They had two small boys and a little girl to bring up, so they decided Colorado was just the place to make their home.

They found some free land in the very heart of the highest mountains. They took up a gold claim on the rugged cliffs of Battle Mountain at an altitude of 10,600 feet. The first year they lived in the tiny settlement of Redcliff, at the foot of the mountain. But they found no gold — only cliffs and an impossible life of hardship.

The next summer they set off for some land at a much lower altitude and much farther west. The land lay west of the tiny settlement of Glenwood Springs in the valley of the Grand River, now known as the Colorado River. This was in 1883, just after the Ute Indians had been "cleared out of Colorado," so there was open homestead land for the taking. As Flora Ann was again expecting another baby in the fall, it was decided that she and the children would camp at Glenwood Springs during the summer while Abram Maxfield rode his horse on west to build an adobe home on their new land.

When he came back to pick up the family in September, he realized he had to dismantle their wagon and pack it in pieces on the backs of horses to cross the high cliffs that rose along the river. The family trailed along behind, climbing the towering cliffs on foot. Ten days after they arrived at the homestead at the mouth of Rifle Creek, Flora Ann had her baby. That baby was my father, Roy Douglas Maxfield, born October 5, 1883.

I have a small ink sketch framed on my living room wall. It is a picture of Glenwood Springs viewed from a cliff above town. My grandmother, Flora Ann, made it just before they left for their homestead. It is dated, in her fine handwriting, Sept. 1883.

That's how close in time Flying Horse Mollie was to my father. Dad was hot on the heels of dear Mollie, although he never knew her as I did. And as for physical proximity, he was born just forty miles by air from the White River Agency.

When my father Roy was nine years old his father died suddenly of a stroke. By this time there were four more children in the family, so Roy, along with the two older boys, had to go out and get a job. To make money and help the family, Roy's mother, Flora Ann, sold off lots to newcomers, thus creating the town of Rifle. Roy's job was riding on the freight wagons that carried freight from the railroad station, which had just been built on the family homestead, over the hills to Meeker, Colorado, once known as the White River Ute Reservation. He helped load and unload the freight and helped with the horses. Many a night the small boy slept along the same trail that the Utes had taken when they fled after the famous Meeker Massacre. He used to tell me of waking up in the morning to find his blanket covered in fresh snow. Mollie had been gone only a short while.

When Roy grew up and fell in love with the beautiful schoolteacher he met in Salt Lake City, what should they do but move back to Ute Indian country in Colorado! They took up a homestead on a mesa near Glenwood Springs and there they lived for the rest of their lives. That's where I grew up, on a beautiful ranch just fifty air miles from Mollie's old home.

Another reason, I think, why I feel so close to Mollie is that I, too, grew up on a horse. She grew up on Moonlight, her snow-white Indian pony, while my little sister and I grew up on old Pat, our beloved sorrel. We grew up wild, as she did, roaming the hills with bobcats

and mountain lions, feeling at one with Mother Earth and Father Sun and all the wild creatures.

After I became "civilized" and graduated from high school in Glenwood Springs, where Chief Colorow used to soak in the magic hot springs, I went away to college, taught school, got married and had two little girls. And then, by the old Ute magic, my family and I were drawn back into the aura of Flying Horse Mollie once more. We settled in Steamboat Springs, where Mollie's Yampa Utes always spent their summers, soaking in their beloved Medicine Springs and racing their ponies in the meadow.

Flying Horse Mollie continues to haunt me. As her people were being "shoved off the face of the Earth" toward the end of her story, I worried also about their hundreds of ponies which they were forced to abandon as the Utes were driven out of Colorado and off into the desolation of Eastern Utah. Like being forced to abandon their children, it was a cruel punishment.

But just this spring, in a copy of the *Steamboat Pilot*, I found the answer to my unsolved question of what happened to the abandoned ponies. Hundreds of them are still running wild in far northwestern Colorado, in the Sandwash country. Every spring the Bureau of Land Management allows "horse runners," experienced western riders, to go into the area and capture as many of the wild ponies as they can. They are sold to buyers who want a wild horse to tame. I wonder if any of Snowball's offspring have been captured yet?

ACKNOWLEDGEMENTS

Even with remarkably close ties with Flying Horse Mollie and her Yampa Utes, I would not have been able to write her story without the assistance of many people. The backing they were able to give me on historical data and the facts concerning the Utes' story were tremendous help.

First let me thank two dear American Indian friends, who, although not Utes, have helped me to understand, admire and respect their culture immensely. One is Tom Willetto, a Navajo who now teaches at an Indian school at Crown Point, New Mexico. I first knew him as a very young man working at the Whiteman School in Steamboat Springs, taking care of the riding program. He is an extremely gifted artist and sculpted a magnificent horse, a statue that was later cast in bronze. He is a remarkably fine man.

The other is Bonnie Jo Hunt, an exquisitely beautiful Hunkpapa Lakota (Standing Rock Sioux) whom I first met many years ago when she was a student of mine in Steamboat Springs. She is a gifted singer and sang for a time with the San Francisco Opera. She is the great-great granddaughter of Chief Mad Bear who fought at the Battle of Little Bighorn. She founded Artists of Indian America, Inc. (AIA), a non-profit organization established to stimulate cultural and social improvement among American Indian youth. To record and preserve her native heritage, in 1997 Bonnie Jo and her husband, Dr. Lawrence J. Hunt, a college professor, launched Mad Bear Press, a press that publishes American history dealing with life on the western frontier. I am proud to say that Bonnie Jo is a beloved and beautiful friend.

Other deeply loved friends have also helped me by unearthing most important information for this book. Among them are Gertrude Fetcher, George Tolles, Glende Martin, Doug Brown and Clela Rorex. George Tolles, Professor of International Relations (ret.) at Colorado Mountain College, loaned his private copy of *The Cabin at Medicine*

Springs by Lulita Pritchett, which was of great assistance in the early chapters of this book. It was Pritchett ancestors, the Crawfords, who are the actual white family in Mollie's story.

Clela Rorex, another precious friend and former student, has been of infinite help to me. She has devoted her life to the betterment of the lives of American Indians by her career as a paralegal with the Native American Rights Fund, headquartered in Boulder, Colorado. Clela gave me the valuable book, *People of the Red Earth: American Indians of Colorado* by Sally Crum.

Among the many others who have given assistance are Peggy Dorr, Librarian at Colorado Mountain College, Alpine Campus, in Steamboat Springs, and Marty Alexandroff of the Tread of the Pioneers Museum, also in Steamboat Springs. This book could not have been completed without their help.

Jan Pettit, whose assistance has been inestimable, should also be thanked. She is the author of the splendid book, *Utes: The Mountain People*. She is also the Executive Director of the Ute Pass Museum and the founder of the Ute Pass Historical Society. She has worked with the Ute people since 1974.

Another who has given me assistance is Larry Cesspooch, a Ute from the Uintah and Ouray Indian Reservation at Fort Duchesne, Utah. He is Director of the Ute Indian Tribal Public Relations there. Recently, working with the local community, he celebrated the dedication of the Ute Monument in Steamboat Springs near the swimming pool with George Tolles officiating. It was designed by Colorow, descendent of the famous Ute of early Meeker days, a suitable tribute.

One of the treasured experiences of my research in producing this book occurred when Joe Sullivan, a fascinating and well-informed "old-timer" of the Meeker area, took my daughter and me out to the Milk Creek Battle Ground and described in detail that part of the story. Here is a man dedicated to the Utes and their history.

Another warm advocate of the Ute cause is Pamela Burwell, on the staff of Colorado Mountain College in Steamboat Springs, who loaned me her copy of *The Last War Trail* by Robert Emmitt, published in 1954.

But I owe my deepest thanks to Marshall Sprague, author of *Massacre: The Tragedy of White River*. I give him special thanks for the use of some quotations from original letters and newspaper articles, to which otherwise I had no access. It is with utmost humility and gratitude that I thank Mr. Sprague for showing me the trail.

* * * * *

(Author's note) *With a bow of gratitude to the Utes and their spiritual beliefs I have capitalized some words not usually capitalized in English, such as East, West, North, South, Nature and Earth, all of which have holy significance to them. I am also capitalizing the words Agent, Agency and Reservation.*

SONG TO THE MOUNTAINS

Mountains loom upon the path we take;
Yonder peak now rises sharp and clear;
Behold! It stands with its head uplifted,
Thither go we, since our way lies there.

Mountains loom upon the path we take;
Yonder peak now rises sharp and clear;
Behold! We climb, draw near its summit;
Steeper grows the way, and slow our steps.

Mountains loom upon the path we take;
Yonder peak that rises sharp and clear;
Behold us now upon its head uplifted;
Planting there our feet, we stand secure.

Mountains loom upon the path we take;
Yonder peak that rose so sharp and clear,
Behold us now upon its head uplifted;
Resting here at last, we sing our song.

                    - Native American chant

Chapter 1

If you will forgive me my little English, I will tell you my story and how we were driven out of our Shining Mountains where the Great Spirit of the Sky planted us forever ago.

Forgive me if I tell it my way, for I never got a chance to learn big words and book talk. I only went to school a short time, and Old Meeker kept me so busy running his errands that I missed a lot of learning.

But I know enough to tell you the whole story and how it really happened. It's an ugly story.

My name is Mollie – Flying Horse Mollie. At least that's what the white folks at the White River Ute Reservation called me then. That's because I loved racing. All Utes loved racing. They worshiped their horses. And they loved betting on the races, too. That was the happiest time of their lives.

I loved riding my Father's ponies. He had a great many good horses, and I nearly always won the race. He was proud of me and my way of winning, so he always let me ride, even though I was the only Ute girl who ever raced.

Maybe the other Utes thought my Father spoiled me, but no one ever said anything. They all knew my Mother died when I was born and that he loved me more than anything else on Earth. Even more than his horses, I think. So he was proud of my racing, and even my White Man's name, Flying Horse Mollie.

I remember it was the Moon-of-Greening-Grass. The Reservation at White River was humming with excitement. We were preparing to welcome a new Agent. The one who had just left did not like Indians. He asked to leave and we were not sad. Maybe the new one would be better. We were hoping.

We Yampa Utes had even more to be excited about. It was the season when we packed up our tipis and all our other possessions, rounded up our horses and headed for the high country. We would be spending most of the summer in the Medicine Springs area, along the Yampa River.

It was our favorite campsite for many reasons. First was the sacred hot springs that bubbled up out of the Earth to ease our elders' aching bones. As soon as we arrived, I knew Little Bear and Lone Eagle would take off their clothes and get into the blessed hot water. We knew the springs were sacred because we could see the breath of the holy ones bubble up through the clear water.

I grew up in the tipi of Little Bear. I never knew my mother who died after my birth. Little Bear was my grandmother and Lone Eagle my grandfather. My father, Thunder Cloud, lived in our tipi, too. But he was too young and healthy to waste time in the sacred waters. He had hunting to do and his great herd of horses to look after.

But down at White River we were glad to get away from our crowd of Ute relatives and into the Blue Sky Mountains again. Another thing we liked about the Medicine Springs park was the racing track where we raced our horses almost every day. The happiest time the Utes ever spend is with our ponies.

We love our ponies more than we love our children. Horses represent life. They represent freedom, and the wind in our faces. They represent beauty. And they represent happiness. We laugh. We shout. We love to bet on the winners. It is the Utes' way of celebrating life.

And another thing we liked about Medicine Springs was that white men had not yet poured into the valley like a flock of ugly grasshoppers. It was still clean and fresh as when the Great Spirit first made it. There was only one family of whites in the valley, and they were no problem. They were friendly and were our good neighbors.

Ma Crawford was the one who taught me to talk in the white man's tongue. I am grateful to her for that. I have never learned how to write their words. But because she taught me to speak, I am now able to tell my story.

I could hear the beat, beat, beat of the drums that morning. It was the beginning of the Bear Dance, one of the most important days of the year, the oldest of all our Ute ceremonies. We had heard the first spring thunder, so we knew it was time for the bears to wake up. The whole world was waking up – the grass, the flowers, the deer, the birds. This was a time of renewal, a time to start a new year.

It made my heart pound with the drum. And I must tell you that I had a special reason to be excited. There was a very special young man, a White River Ute, who would be dancing. He was a beautiful young man, Morning Star, who was helping arrange the celebration to honor the women. I hoped I could get him to dance with me.

I slipped into my special white doeskin dress and rushed out the flaps of our tipi. Little Bear and Lone Eagle had already gone and Thunder Cloud was long ago busy with his ponies.

I hurried across the wide meadow to the circle of the brush corral that the men had been building for the dance. The opening was to the East to greet the rising sun, just as our tipis were. The sun is sacred, you know.

I entered the circle. Several of the older women were kneeling on blankets, playing games with deer-bone dice. The dancing had not yet begun. But the musicians were set around their echo chamber with their notched sticks in hand, ready to start their rhythmic thrumming.

My eyes found Morning Star. He pretended to be busy talking with someone else. It was time to choose a partner. I walked over to the men and, pretending I didn't care, flicked him with the end of my sash. He rose and followed me to the center of the circle. The old women hurried to pick up their dice and blankets. The dance began. My partner didn't look at me.

Others had joined us, the men in a line facing the East, and the women in a line facing them. We began jogging, two steps forward and three steps back. Two steps forward, three steps back. And at the end of the lines was the Cat Man, dressed up in all his finery. He made sure our lines were straight and that we didn't bump each other. Sometimes he did things to make us laugh. He was really Canalla, our Chief Medicine Man. We all liked him.

The steady rhythm of the musicians went on and on. Four days we danced, with the thrumming of the rubbing sticks against the notched "bear-growlers" echoing across the meadow. On the fourth day the music went on until somebody fell down. It was a test of strength between the men and women. As the sun was turning red over the trees in the West, someone fell. It was a woman at the other end of the line. The men had won.

And then we feasted. And feasted. And laughed. And thanked the Great Spirit that we had survived another bitter winter and were about to start the new year.

I didn't see Morning Star again. But I thought of him often.

Thunder Cloud was impatient to be on the trail for the Shining Mountains to the northeast, the land of Medicine Springs.

"We must be leaving soon!" he kept repeating, even before Grandmother and Grandfather were out of their beds. They were old and the four days of celebration had made them very tired. Poor Lone Eagle groaned under his buffalo robe, listening to Father's urging as he stamped around the tipi, trying to get us roused.

I, too, would rather have slept later into the morning. After those long endless days of the Bear Dance, my legs still ached. But my heart pounded with the joy of the dance and the echo of the drums in my head. It was a wonderful day to be young and alive.

"We must be on the trail!"

"Yes, Father." I hurried into my dark worn buckskin dress. I carefully folded my white doeskin dress I'd worn for the dancing and packed it into my little parfleche, the rawhide box where I kept all my belongings.

"Can you and Grandmother strike the tipi if I go out to round up my herd now?"

"Yes, Father. I always do, you know."

"You won't let them go back to sleep?"

"No, Father." I took a piece of elk jerky out of the food box and began to chew it. I had to prove that I was really wide awake. I was eager to be on the trail, too, but not as much as he was.

"Can you and Little Bear handle the lodge poles alone, Little One?" I knew I was his pet, since I was the only child he had, but I was no baby.

"You know I can, Thunder Cloud," I answered him with great dignity. That showed him I wanted to be called by my real name, Flying Horse.

"Very well." He swallowed the last of his jerky and turned to open the flaps of the tipi. "I go to round up the ponies now."

Thunder Cloud was the richest Ute in the Yampa band. We counted our wealth in ponies, which numbered more than fifty.

"Please bring in Moonlight first, so we can get the travois loaded," I called after him.

Moonlight was my own pony. She was the most beautiful horse in the world – snow white, with long fast legs, a coat like white doeskin and a head like a flying bird. And her eyes! Big and black, they looked into your very heart. Oh, how I worshiped her! All Utes dearly loved their ponies, but I more than most, I think. I would have given my very life for her.

Thunder Cloud gave her to me when I was four years old and she was just a tiny foal. We grew up together. And she knew what I said, I know. I kept her clean and shining, brushing her daily.

I rushed out when I heard Father bring her up. I threw my arms around her neck. I hadn't seen her for four day. She lowered her head to my shoulder and nickered softly. This was her way of saying "Good morning."

I pressed my cheek to hers and then hurried back to help Little Bear get our buffalo robes packed up. Before long we had all we owned in a neat pile before the tipi. Lone Eagle had at last got his aching bones out of his bed and was chewing his jerky.

Then we struck the tipi. It wasn't easy with just the two of us. I was getting stronger and taller each year, but Little Bear was getting smaller and weaker. All Ute tipis belong to the women, and it was our job to take them down and put them up again.

Other Yampa Utes were also striking their tipis and getting ready to head for the Blue Sky Country so the area around the Agency headquarters was in a big hubbub. Moonlight stood quietly while I tied the eight lodge poles on her withers, four to a side. Her head was high, and her ears pricked up with the excitement.

Then both Little Bear and Lone Eagle helped me rope the folded tipi to the poles behind Moonlight's heels. We were ready to go.

Quinket and his family, who had their tipi next to ours all winter, had already hit the trail. Quinket was the leader of the Yampa band and it was proper that he should lead the way, even though we knew it by heart since we had traveled it so many times. And besides, the many travois going to Medicine Springs had cut a trail in the earth that a blind man could have followed. In fact, it is still there in many places, and white men have even built their roads upon it, using our old Ute trail.

I could see Thunder Cloud out East of the Agency, trying to keep his ponies rounded up while he waited for us. And I seemed to see a thundercloud over his face, showing his impatience to be on the way. I had to hurry.

But still I delayed. I was so much hoping that I would see Morning Star again. I scanned the area of the Agency, hoping for a last glimpse of him. I had been hoping that he might come by to tell me goodbye. Hadn't he enjoyed dancing with me for four long suns? And he knew I would be gone from the White River Agency all summer. My heart was heavy. Did he like me? Would he remember me when I left? Would he dance with me next year at the Bear Dance? I couldn't tell, because he had not spoken to me. But he was shy and oh, so beautiful!

Little Bear and Lone Eagle had already climbed with some difficulty onto their little pinto ponies. "Come, little one!" Lone Eagle urged. They all still thought of me as a little child, their baby. "Thunder Cloud will not wait!"

I leaped onto Moonlight's back so fast she jumped a little. We were on our way. We were on the trail to Medicine Springs and the Shining Mountains.

Chapter 2

After we got started, there seemed to be no rush. The ponies were hungry after a long hard winter and often paused to snatch a bite of the moist green grass that was beginning to grow tall along the creek bottoms. The land was arid in many places, so the horses took every chance to pause for a mouthful of fresh food when they found it.

The way was long, very long. But I was riding my beloved Moonlight, and so my spirits began to rise a little. When we found a large patch of grass, we would stop for a rest and let the old folks dismount and stretch their stiffened legs. We would be many days along the trail.

Little Bear rummaged in the rawhide box where we kept our food. It was our first stop and we were all hungry. While the ponies grazed along the river bottom, we enjoyed a good piece of pemmican from Grandmother's food box that traveled on her little travois.

As I chewed the tasty lunch, I remembered making it last year. I remembered picking the serviceberries along the hills beside the upper Yampa. I remembered pounding them with the fired venison that we had prepared from the many deer that Thunder Cloud had shot while he hunted across the Flattops during the past summer. I loved pemmican. It was better than jerky.

I watched the sky, the clouds seeming to play leapfrog in the spring winds that swept across the hills. They moved and shifted and changed color, from white to black, from gray to the color of wild grapes.

Suddenly my eye caught a different color, a rising cloud of dust puffing up on the trail behind us. Another band of horses was coming and coming fast.

Our ponies pricked up their ears and whinnied. Who was coming? As the newcomers got nearer I recognized Storm riding hard. Storm was another Yampa Ute, heading for Medicine Springs.

Thunder Cloud had seen him, too. He stood and raised his hand in greeting.

"Hi-yah!" he shouted. "Why do you run?"

"I get the best camping spot on the race tracks at Medicine Springs!" Storm shouted back, not slowing down as his small band of ponies thundered past.

"He has no regard for his ponies, "Thunder Cloud frowned, shaking his head. "He wants always to be the winner. Even though he kills his ponies in winning." I knew Father didn't like Storm very much.

* * * * *

The first night out, we made an easy, makeshift camp along the river bottom where the ponies could have a good night's pasture. We spread our beds under a slight bluff nearby, out of the wind. Lone Eagle built a fire and Little Bear had gone to the river to bring back her cooking-basket of water to boil. At the Reservation we had learned to enjoy a cup of hot coffee after a hard day. We had managed to trade a doeskin for a small packet of the magic seeds.

Tonight was a good time to boil a few. We were still weary from the activities of the long Bear Dance. And today had been a long day.

Little Bear had just gotten out our sheep-horn mugs when we heard the shrill whinny of a horse out of the western darkness. Our band of ponies answered the stranger over the hill. A lone rider emerged from the night. He leaped from his horse beside our fire.

It was Morning Star.

"Greetings!" he said. "I was in hopes I might overtake you."

My family stared at him in surprise. White River Utes did not go on our summer hunting expeditions with the Yampa Utes. But here he was! My heart pounded, and my face was suddenly hot.

He untied a small bundle from the back of his horse.

"I went hunting before you left the Reservation this morning, but you had gone before I got back." He flopped the bundle on the earth at Thunder Cloud's feet.

"I thought you would like some fresh venison for your trip," he mumbled. Knowing how shy he was, I knew he was embarrassed by his speech. Dear, beautiful Morning Star! "My shame is great. All I could bring you is this jack rabbit." His face was flushed.

"Towaoc!" said Thunder Cloud. "Thanks!" He tried not to look surprised.

Morning Star sat on his heels and stared into the fire.

"Hunting is not good on the White River," he spoke softly. "Finding any game took me long time."

Thunder Cloud nodded. Could this meager gift mean marriage?

"Let's hope it's better on the Flat Tops."

Little Bear handed the young man a steaming mug. He raised his eyebrows in surprise.

"Coffee," she said. "It will take your weariness away."

"Thanks." He gulped the hot drink gratefully.

But Utes do not waste their time with empty words.

"Flying Horse," Thunder Cloud turned to me, "get an extra pad for Morning Star. He can sleep here beside the fire."

I got out an ancient buffalo hide and patted it into place in the ring of firelight. I cast him a welcoming glance, but he didn't see it. He was still looking into the fire. Did he know I was alive? Did he care?

The next morning when we awoke, he was gone. He was probably nearing the Reservation by now. Again my spirit was low.

* * * * *

As we climbed higher into the Yampa Valley, the high waters of Spring raged deeper and more dangerous. In many places they filled the entire valley, even burying the fresh grass under lakes from thunder in many places.

I began to notice another thing. Moonlight was beginning now to tire more easily. I knew she had a baby colt in her belly. Thunder Cloud had told me so. But we weren't expecting it to come until we had settled in at Medicine Springs up in the valley. I began to worry about my precious Moonlight.

More and more she lagged behind the others, and I had to keep kicking her in the ribs in order to keep up. She wanted to stop often, not to snatch grass as the other ponies did but to stop and puff. She was always out of breath.

Suddenly a more urgent problem rose up ahead of us. The sky to the East suddenly darkened. Storm clouds began to rise up out of the Shining Mountains. No thunder, as we could expect in this Moon-of-Greening-Grass but only fierce clouds, blackening the sky with a kind of terror that chilled me to my very bone.

Snow clouds! Snow? Here in spring? I refused to think of the possibility. Instead I tried to worry about Moonlight. But the icy winds cutting down off the far distant Flat Tops tore through my buckskin dress. I shuddered and pulled my blanket higher around my shoulders.

I could see Lone Eagle and Little Bear ahead of me, their old shoulders humped deep into their blankets as they plodded on. They were freezing, too, I knew. I looked back over my shoulder to locate Thunder Cloud. He was far back in the rear, driving his great herd of ponies along against the bitter wind. Only he was hardy enough not to untie his blanket yet. Or maybe he was just too anxious to get his herd to safety to care.

I heard a distant shout. I looked back. He was making urgent motions to stop.

Soon he was riding beside me.

"We must camp here!" He was frowning so I knew he was worried. "The snow will hit us before night. We can't go on!"

And he galloped ahead, overtaking the others. Moonlight stopped, panting heavily. The old ones turned slowly and came back to where I waited, Thunder Cloud with them.

"Not a good place to camp," growled Lone Eagle. "No pasture for horses."

"Forget horses for now!" Thunder Cloud's voice carried a strange urgency. "We must help the women pitch the tipi or we will all perish! It will be a bitter night!"

Hurriedly we untied my travois from Moonlight's quivering withers and set up the lodge poles. It went much faster with the four of us working. But with all the strength we had, it was almost more than we could do to pull up the heavy elk-skin tipi, for the terrible wind tore it out of our hands more than once.

I was still pounding in the ground pegs around the edge when the storm hit us. Instantly the wind drove icy wet arrows of snow into our eyes, our noses, and into our very lungs.

The great herd of ponies behind us moved into a tight knot, turning their tails to the fierce wind. No need of pasture tonight. They couldn't have found it if it had been under their very feet.

I tethered Moonlight nearby with a ground peg, and we all hurried into the tipi and tied the flaps tight behind us. It didn't take us long to take out our beds and crawl into them. Although the terrific force of the snow could not reach us, we hadn't had time to gather any wood for a fire. The tipi seemed colder than during the Moon-of-Frozen-Breath back on the Reservation.

I pulled the buffalo robe over my head and shuddered. I would never be warm again. The wind screamed and whistled around the tipi. The gods of the storm were very angry with us that night. What had we done to set them off, I wondered. I prayed that the lodge poles would remain upright. What if they collapsed on top of us? Would the weight of the tipi kill us? Would the blow of a lodge pole to his head kill even Thunder Cloud?

And what of Moonlight? And all the other ponies? Would they survive this night? I wished desperately that I could have brought Moonlight into the tipi with us. Poor beautiful Moonlight! And she sick besides.

In spite of my terror, I somehow drifted off to sleep during the night. I think the silence awakened me. I jerked the buffalo robe from my face and sat up. Dawn was brightening the Eastern side of the tipi. The others were still asleep. They had probably stayed awake most of the night, as I had.

I jumped up and untied the flaps as fast as my fingers would move. Was the storm over? At least that roaring wind had died. The sun was beginning to come up. I was blinded by the brilliance. The storm was gone. A dazzling blue sky sang above the endless snow that buried the Earth.

I squinted against the sun, searching for Moonlight. She was gone! I waded out into the deep snow; my heart seemed to burst in my chest with deafening force. Gone? But where? I rushed around behind the tipi.

There she stood. I saw the blood across the snow first. Blood? I thought for a moment I would faint.

And then I saw it! A tiny foal tottered beside her. His long legs wobbled uncertainly. His soft little nose nuzzled around beneath his mother's belly, searching for food.

Moonlight turned and looked over her shoulder, nickering at me softly.

"Thunder Cloud!" I cried. "Little Bear! Lone Eagle! Come see! We have a baby!"

Chapter 3

Thunder Cloud announced that we would stay in camp for a couple of days, so we began gathering wood. He didn't say whether we stayed because of the snow banks ahead of us or because he thought Moonlight needed to rest before another long day with the travois. I think it was Moonlight he was concerned with. Utes worship their horses. We consider them sacred. Our very lives depend on them.

While the Spring sun quickly melted the snow, the Yampa River climbed higher along its banks. We were just below a narrow canyon, where the cliffs crowded close on either side and the foaming Spring flood gushed forth with a deafening roar. How would we ever cross to the North side? That's where we wanted to be when we got to Medicine Springs.

I spent my time with Moonlight and the tottering colt. I named him Snowball and spent the day stroking his tiny velvet nose whenever he allowed it. His head was tucked beneath his mother's flank most of the time. He seemed to be ravenous. And I could see him getting stronger and more independent by the hour.

By the third day, when we packed up and set out again, he was frisking around like a young puppy, full of vigor and play. And he was intelligent, too, and as smart as his mother. I'm sure he was already beginning to recognize his name. Oh, what a beautiful little pony he was! I couldn't have been happier.

Whereas Moonlight was snowy white except for her gray velvet nose, Snowball was a deeper gray in color, almost black. But I knew his coat would lighten as he grew older. Moonlight's had, I remembered.

By the end of the second sun, we had reached Medicine Springs. The sunset was spilling a vivid pink across the high mountain before us. It was a mountain of wild roses in bloom, I thought. It was good to be home again.

"Can you hear it?" I asked Lone Eagle.

"Hear what?" I knew his bones were filled with pain, for he carried the pain in his face.

"The Talking Spring. Can't you hear it?"

"Of course I can hear it!" He sounded angry but I knew he wasn't, just tired. My grandmother and grandfather were never angry with me. They never had been. They loved me too much. They meant everything to me. They were my mother, whom I had never known, and my father, who was too busy with his great herd of ponies to spend much time with me.

I was so happy to be home, I kept on chattering. The Talking Spring continued to chug-chug-chug up ahead of us.

"What is it that white man calls it? A strange word."

"Steamboat Springs. Even the Utes know that word."

"What does it mean?"

"It means Iron-Horse-on-the-River. White men who lived far, far into the sunrise have these strange creatures riding on the wide rivers, they tell me. And they speak like our Talking Spring."

I loved that familiar sound. Chug-chug-chug. It meant home.

Little Snowball was getting tired, I knew. Two long days for those young legs was more than enough. He had begun to lag behind. But the big herd behind us raised their heads to the wind and whinnied. They could smell the other Ute ponies up ahead, around the bend in the cliff, although we still weren't near enough to see them.

Thunder Cloud decided to make temporary camp here by the – what was it? Steamboat Springs? Iron-Horse-on-the-River. The Yampa River was still too high and dangerous to try to cross tonight. Its raging water would subside somewhat during the night, a brief break from the high waters of melting snow. We would drive the big herd across to the north side to get around the high cliff barring our way to the racetracks.

By sunrise we were ready to attempt the crossing. It would be dangerous, we knew, but easier than climbing the mountain above the cliff and coming in by Sulphur Cave. Thunder Cloud would drive the big herd across first, although he knew they would fight against entering the roaring river.

"I'll go ahead, Father, and lead the way. I've done it before, you know."

"Yes," he frowned, "and lose Snowball in the high water! No! I can't allow it."

"Please, why not, Father? I'll tie Snowball's head to my belt. It's the only way. The water is already beginning to rise. Please!"

He looked at me doubtfully. "He still thinks I'm a little girl," I said to myself. "He must begin to realize I'm a woman!"

"But you'll have to come back and get your favorite travois and tipi!" he argued.

"I know. That's why we must hurry!" I begged him with my eyes.

At last he nodded. "Very well, little Flying Horse. I'll hold Snowball at the racetrack with the herd." Keeping Snowball's head close to Moonlight's flank, I drove her quickly into the river with my sharp heels. Always obedient to my commands, she jumped into the roaring water and swam with frightened vigor. I held little Snowball's head close and snug under my arm. The great herd, with Thunder Cloud whooping behind them, followed suit.

As Moonlight lunged up on to the dry bank, I looked up. There was the Crawfords' log cabin just above us. And in front stood the family, watching us. The children were hopping up and down in excitement and clapping their hands. Ma and Pa clapped their hands and cheered.

But we couldn't stop now with the other horses charging up the bank behind us. We had to move on, fast. We had to lead the herd back across the river at the racetrack, and then come back for my travois, and finally help Little Bear and Lone Eagle with their crossing.

"A colt! A colt!" I could hear Little John shouting in his wild excitement.

But I had to ride on. No stopping now. We must cross again.

The area around the racetrack was a whole village of tipis, camped in a large circle in the flat valley. It was a welcome sight. I could recognize Storm's tipi. And there was Yahmonite's tipi. He was our best friend among the Yampa Utes. He was a fine man. His little son Charlie ran out to meet us. It was wonderful to be with our own.

It was sundown again before we had our tipi pitched and our buffalo robes in place for our beds. I had crossed the angry Yampa eight times that day! Eight times! I felt at that moment that I would always be struggling against those treacherous currents. But I had done it. And I had won! Thunder Cloud was proud.

Poor little Snowball was starving. There hadn't been time for him to get a decent meal all day, poor baby. Now Moonlight was tethered beside our tipi and Snowball nursed in ecstasy, butting his head against her belly occasionally to get the milk flowing faster.

I think maybe this was the happiest time of the year for the Yampa Utes. They were home. This was their valley. They would spend the summer doing the two things they loved most – hunting and racing. There was no place on Earth like this Yampa Valley, we were sure.

The Great Spirit always smiled down on us from his home in the Sun. All his creatures were in perfect harmony – the two-leggeds, the four-leggeds, the winged, and the rooted. They were just as he had intended us to live when he created us. I went to sleep that night in Little Bear's tipi as happy as I had ever been. I would cross the river again tomorrow to visit the Crawfords.
* * * * *

More Yampa families were crossing the river the next day, coming close on our heels. We hadn't traveled together because each herd of horses needed all the pasture they would get each night, so we were all strung out along the trail from the White River Agency. Wouldn't it have been wonderful if Nature's harmony had reigned on the White River as it did along the Yampa?

Thunder Cloud was out early, although the horses were still too weary from the long trip to start racing today. That would come later. The men were all glad to get together, to talk about the trail along the river and about any adventures along the way.

Lone Eagle would have to wait for a few days for the high water to fall a little before he could get back across the river to his sacred hot springs. But he was here, and it wouldn't be long. He and Little Bear could wait.

As I came out of our tipi, I heard Thunder Cloud laughing hilariously. What has set him off, I wondered? Storm, too, was doubled with laughter. Then I recognized the pony of White Trader. That explained it. He was probably passing out drinks of firewater to the Utes. Thunder Cloud didn't drink, so I wasn't worried. But Storm did, unfortunately. I hated to see the Trader and his barrel of firewater. It made some Utes crazy, really crazy.

I was on my way to the Crawfords' cabin, so I brushed any worry thoughts aside. Today was a beautiful day.

Ma Crawford and Lulita were delighted to see me. The boys, Logan and John, were off fishing, as usual, but both Ma and Lulita threw their arms around me. I tethered Moonlight.

"Come in! Come in!" Ma cried. "Pa has just come back from Georgetown with a load of supplies, and he brought us a treat I'll bet you'll love as much as we do!"

"Let's not tell her, Ma!" Lulita said. "Let's let it be a big surprise!" Lulita was probably two or three years younger than I, so I felt she was still a little girl. But she was a dear child and always full of excitement. I was really fond of her.

Ma was busy at the cupboard and at the iron stove where they cooked or heated their food. Soon she brought me a white china cup, steaming and fragrant. What was it? I wondered. White people had such strange ways.

"What is it?" I sniffed it again.

"Try it and see!" Lulita almost squealed in delight.

I took a long sip. Delicious! Never had I tasted anything like it. "What is it?" I asked again.

"Cocoa! Isn't it grand?" Lulita wanted me to like it. And I did. I drank and drank until the cup was empty. "More," I said, holding out my cup. I didn't know many white man's words, but I knew that. And it showed I liked it.

We had a great day. They taught me lots of new words and told me I had a "remarkable memory," whatever that meant. I guess it meant they thought I was doing fine. We laughed and had much fun.

When it was time for me to leave, they followed me down to the riverbank and asked me to come back again soon. Then I rode up the trail to the upper crossing, waving them good-by. I wish now that day had never happened. But unaware, I crossed the Yampa again, with Snowball's little head under my arm, as it had been yesterday morning.

C h a p t e r   4

When Thunder Cloud entered the tipi that night, I thought he was sick. His face was very pale. He held on to the center pole for support.

"Flying Horse, little daughter, I have some sad news for you."

"What is it, Father?" What news could he possible have? News? From where?

"It is a very sad story." His face was buried in his chest. "Very sad. Very, very sad."

What on Earth?

"I must take Moonlight over to Storm's camp."

"Why? Now? Tonight?"

"Moonlight is Storm's pony now."

My heart choked in my throat. Horror sent me reeling. I felt as sick as Thunder Cloud looked at this moment.

"Why, Thunder Cloud?" I managed to whisper. "Why?"

"The shame is mine." I could see two tears making their way down his brown cheeks. But I was too stunned to wonder at this strange sight. "And my shame is great," he went on.

I sat silent. I had no words. Little Bear and Lone Eagle were as speechless as I was. At last Thunder Cloud spoke. We could scarcely hear him.

"White Trader was giving the Utes firewater. I said no. I hate the stuff. But everyone laughed and teased me. They said 'No hunting today. Why not fire water?' So I took a cup, I am ashamed to say." He could not go on. I could not remain silent.

"Thunder Cloud, you didn't!" Anger began to boil up in me. "You didn't give Moonlight to Storm! You couldn't!"

"Worse than that, daughter. I played dice with him. I lost."

I broke into tears. I could not help it. I had not cried in all my life that I remembered. For a time I cried so hard I could not talk. Finally I spoke.

"How could you? Moonlight is mine! Mine!"

He raised his head and spoke firmly.

"All the ponies in my herd are mine!"

"No, Thunder Cloud!" I yelled at him. "She is mine! Mine! Do you hear? Mine! You gave her to me!"

"Yes. But you are mine, too, you know. I have the right."

I lunged at him and started beating him on the chest. I, who had always been such a good and obedient daughter. I was striking my father!

"No, dear child," I heard Lone Eagle's voice behind me, soft and gentle. "Thunder Cloud is right, you know. The ponies are his."

I flew out the door of our tipi, not looking back. I jerked Moonlight's tether pin loose and leaped on her back, my heels kicking her ribs. I headed for the river crossing, a startled Snowball at our heels. Not slowing down, I grabbed Snowball's short tether rope and dragged him close as we plunged into the Yampa River.

I was going back to the Crawfords' cabin. I didn't care if I never saw another Ute again as long as I lived. Treacherous! I had lost faith in my father, in my tribe...forever. Moonlight's hoofs thundered West with little Snowball racing along behind as fast as his tiny hoofs could go.

"Please!" I slid off Moonlight's back and into Ma Crawford's arms. "Please! I stay here? Tonight?"

She held me back and stared into my tear-wet face.

"What in the world has happened? Are you all right?"

"Please? I stay?" I was afraid I would start crying again.

"Yes. Yes, of course," she kissed me gently on the cheek. "Come on in. But you must tell me what happened." With her arm around my shoulders, we went into the cabin.

It was warm and fragrant with the smell of cooking food. I was sickened by the smell. I slumped into a chair and buried my face in my arms on the table.

"Run away." I searched for the white man's words. "No go home. Never."

Ma Crawford busied herself around the stove. Then she set a steaming cup of what was it— cocoa? — on the table before me.

"Drink this. And then we can talk a little."

In spite of my misery, I drank the wonderful drink.

"Now, dear girl, tell me what happened." She put her warm hand over mine.

Again I hunted for the proper words in a strange tongue.

"Thunder Cloud. My father. He drink firewater. White Trader. He play dice. He lose my horse. My Moonlight. Mine forever. I never go home. Never again."

"Oh, you poor girl!" I saw sudden tears in her eyes, too. She squeezed my hand. Then she got up and was again busy around the stove. "We must talk to Pa."

Suddenly the Crawford boys came pounding into the kitchen, both talking at the top of their voices, each trying to out shout the other.

"Ma! Guess what! A Ute pony is here! Just outside the door! And she has a colt!"

"Yes, I know," she answered quietly, casting a look in my direction. Then they saw me.

"Oh, hello! It's you! And the colt is yours?"

"Yes..." Then I remembered. I shook my head. "No. Storm's colt. Storm's Moonlight." I dropped my face into my arms again.

"Never mind now. We'll talk about it when Pa gets back from hunting. Put your buckets of milk in the milk shed and get washed up for supper. Where's Lulita?"

"She's feeding the calf its milk," said Logan, as he went out the door. I could feel him staring at me in wide curiosity.

"Can I pet your colt?" Little John asked me as he started out with his milk bucket.

I nodded. Lulita came in and stopped short on seeing me. She could see I'd been crying.

"What's the matter, Ma?" she whispered.

"Never mind now, dear. We'll talk about it when Pa gets home."

It was after dark when Pa got in with his buck and hung it up in the shed. He'd skin it out tomorrow, he said. At least they would eat for a while.

"Evening, miss!" He looked startled to see me huddled at the supper table. "How is everything going?"

I shook my head. I couldn't speak.

"Pa," Ma rushed in. "Flying Horse is in some sad trouble. Her father lost her horse in a poker game today. Is there anything we can do to help?"

"Well, now..." Pa scratched his head and helped himself to some fried potatoes and the last of the fried venison. I could see he was troubled, thinking.

"She says she's never going home again. What shall we do?"

It was so quiet you could hear a feather drop in a forest.

"I think I'd better go over to the Ute camp first thing in the morning and have a little talk with Yahmonite. I know him better than any of the others. I don't want to cause any trouble with the Utes by getting involved in a family affair."

"Can she stay here tonight, then?"

"She can sleep with me!" interrupted Lulita. "There's lots of room in my bed!" I could see that she was delighted and was back to her usual laughing self.

"Can I go out and feed Moonlight a bucket of oats?" asked Logan. "I'll bet she's starved!"

"Great idea, Son!"

"Can I go out and pet the colt?" John looked from me to his father.

"Sure!" Pa agreed. I nodded.

"What's his name?" John asked.

"Snowball," I said in white man's tongue. I had already asked the same question of Lone Eagle, who knew a few words.

"Snowball!" exploded John. "But he's black! Why Snowball?"

I shrugged. I didn't know enough words.

"I'll bet I know!" laughed Lulita. "I'll bet he was born during that big snow storm we had last week."

"Not a very good name for a black pony," sniffed John.

"But black colts sometimes turn white as they grow up, you know. He may be as white as his mother some day."

*****

Next morning, before the river began to rise, Yahmonite was there in front of the Crawford cabin. But he wasn't alone. Lone Eagle was there, too, still astride his pony. I was already out, brushing down Moonlight's shiny coat with Logan's currycomb.

"Hayah," Lone Eagle greeted me. He looked very tired and very, very old. I felt sorry for him. He was still dripping from the river. I knew that gave his bones a greater ache than ever.

But I did not speak.

"Thunder Cloud is feeling a very deep shame today," he spoke in our own tongue. "He wants you to return to us."

"I cannot, dear Lone Eagle. I cannot forgive him."

"But he had the right to play dice."

"Not with Moonlight! Moonlight is my life! I cannot live without her! I will never let her go to Storm!"

"But the whole herd belongs to Thunder Cloud, you know." He was gentle, but he was firm. I knew I could not change his mind.

"You stay here with white people, Thunder Cloud lose face with Utes."

"And I shall be glad. Glad!"

"Storm will cause trouble if you do not give Moonlight."

"Never!"

Lone Eagle sat his horse, the ache cutting deep lines in his face. He looked at me a long time. Then, calmly, without more words, he took Moonlight's tether rope and led her to the crossing.

A knife struck my very soul. Deep, so deep but I loved my dear grandfather. I could not attack him as I had Thunder Cloud. I wanted only to die. I would go to our Home in the Sky. Tonight. And there I would have my Moonlight again. And Snowball. I watched Lone Eagle cross the rising river, with Moonlight and Snowball close behind.

The Great Spirit must help, I prayed aloud. I held my breath, watching, watching. Watching all three horses fighting the current. Quickly they were swept downstream. Down. Down. The colt's head was under water more than it was out. I screamed, silently.

At last I saw Lone Eagle's pony clambering up the opposite bank, Moonlight behind him. But Snowball was swept around the bend in the river and out of sight.

For a moment, the world went black, as black as midnight. When I could see again, I saw Logan racing down our side of the river. I hadn't known a young boy could run that fast. Soon he too was out of sight.

All of us at the cabin were silent. No one made a sound. I was screaming inside, but no one could hear me. There was nothing we could say.

Ages passed in that terrible silence in which we were frozen. Suddenly a strange sight appeared. At first I could not imagine what it was. Then I realized it was Logan. He moved just one staggering step at a time and then laid the limp black thing on the ground.

It was Snowball!

We all raced to Logan's assistance.

"Is he alive?" shouted Lulita.

"Yes! I can hear him breathe!"

Chapter 5

Together we all lifted Snowball and allowed the river water to drain from his lungs. I was little help. I was still so faint I could scarcely stand.

But he was breathing. We could see the slight rise and fall of his waterlogged hide. I kept petting him and crooning to him, the same cradlesong Little Bear used to sing to me. I refused to join the family when they went to meals. I was not hungry. I wanted only to be with Snowball. I sat cross-legged on the Earth with his tiny head in my lap. I sang and petted, sang and petted.

Suddenly, as the setting sun was casting a rosy glow across the West, Snowball's head jerked erect. He looked around, staring about as though still frightened, still fighting the current.

"Snowball's alive!" shouted John, who had been sitting patiently at my side all afternoon.

The family came running. They all clapped and cheered in their joy, the joy they shared with me. I hugged Snowball's head to me. He leaped to his feet, still staggering a little. At least, I still had my colt.

Lulita patted my shoulder, showing her love.

"We're going out to the corral to milk the cows now," she whispered. "When I get back, I'll show you how to teach Snowball to drink milk out of a bucket."

He staggered around a little and nickered for his mother.

"She's gone, little pet," I tried to soothe him, tried to stroke him. "She's gone...forever!" But he would not stand still. He was as devastated as I was. We were both crazy with grief. He continued to nicker like a poor wild thing.

When Lulita came back, she dumped a part of her milk into a small bucket. "Let's go to the barn," she said. "It will be easier there."

Logan and John half dragged, half shoved him down to the barn. Once inside, Lulita tried to explain what she was going to do, but I couldn't understand her. "Hold him," she told the boys. "I'll show her how we teach the calves to drink."

She shoved his head down into the bucket and held it there while inserting her two forefingers in his mouth. He struggled fiercely, but she persisted. Suddenly he tasted the warm sweet milk, a little like his mother's milk. It was good. The fingers on his tongue felt like his mother's teats, the source of that milk. He began to nurse, ravenously. His stomach was hollow and crying for food. Slowly Lulita pulled her fingers from his mouth. He kept on sucking the milk up. Logan and John looked at each other, grinning with satisfaction. Snowball would live!

My heart went out to this white family. They were so good! For a moment, I wondered why the Utes distrusted the whites so much. Even Lone Eagle, so old and wise, always said, "They speak with wicked tongues. They lie. Always lie. When Utes promise, that promise is forever. Like our Shining Mountains. Forever."

But as the summer wore on, I began to realize the many differences in our ways. The constant chattering of the children wore on my nerves. I longed for the peace and quiet of our tipis and the soft gentle talk of the elders. I hadn't realized how much I enjoyed the deep warm murmuring of the men around the campfire in the evenings as they recounted their adventures of the day, such as the big elk one had shot up on Buffalo Pass or the difficulties encountered in trying to locate a buffalo herd. Game was getting scarce. Not like it used to be in the old days. Not like it was when they crossed over into North Park. It must be because of the white man.

Here, at the Crawfords, it seemed to be only noise and senseless racket. As the days passed, I longed to get back with the tribe. The thing of camping forever in one spot was wearing on me. Too, I yearned to get on a pony — to ride, ride, and ride with the wind in my face.

I remembered the quiet arguments between Little Bear and Thunder Cloud about this very thing.

"She must remain with me, here at the tipi," my grandmother used to insist. "She must learn to be a woman! She must learn the ways of a woman! She cannot remain a naughty boy all her life!"

But Thunder Cloud had no son. He liked to have me ride with him on his hunts, even though other women never did such things - not unless they were taken along to butcher and skin the game for the men. He was proud of me, I knew. Thunder Cloud continued to take me with him when he was scouting for game.

Thunder Cloud was also supremely proud of my racing ability. He often bet on Moonlight and me and usually won. I longed to be back in the Shining Mountains again with him, not here on this dried-up hillside in a smelly cabin.

I wished that things were as they had been. But I couldn't face Thunder Cloud now. He had betrayed me. I couldn't forget it. But, as time went on, I began to realize that he had done nothing wrong in the Utes' eyes. It was true. The entire herd of ponies was his, his to dispose of as he saw fit.

My mind told me he was right. But my aching heart rebelled. I couldn't go back. Not now.

But one thing was good. I was learning to speak the white man's tongue. I couldn't help it. It rattled around me every hour of the day it seemed. Lulita whispered it to me the last thing at night, and I could hear Ma and Pa talking before we were even up in the mornings. Caw-caw-caw-caw. They were like a flock of magpies.

John and I spent most of our time with Snowball. He soon became his happy rollicking self again, galloping around the cabin like a young puppy, his little tail straight in the air. But he was still terrified of the river. He wouldn't go near it unless I dragged him, which I did two or three times a day to get a drink of water. He needed that. Even though the spring water had gone down and it now flowed past with a crystal clear murmur, he was afraid. He always would be, I knew.

I thought of Thunder Cloud constantly. I knew by now that he had gone on with most of the tribe up the Yampa River and up on to the Flat Tops, shining in the South, still white with snow. Early spring hunting was always difficult, as the animals were still hungry from the long winter. And the females of every family were all busy producing and suckling their young. Hunting at this season always meant stalking the biggest bull elk or biggest buck deer. Oh, how I longed to be with my father where I belonged!

Or maybe he had decided to cross over Buffalo Pass to North Park to seek out the last of the dwindling buffalo that still roamed in the more remote places. We needed some buffalo skin so badly. Our tipis were old and shabby. Our beds were wearing thin and hard. Elk hides just weren't warm enough for bitter winter weather.

And how was my beautiful, beloved Moonlight? Was Storm treating her well? I doubted it. Of all the band of Utes, Storm was the harshest with his string of ponies. My poor, dear Moonlight! I longed to be astride her, with her lovely white mane flying in the wind as I raced. Did Storm ever comb and brush her? Of course he didn't.

I often walked away from the cabin, trying to be alone. But little John was always there with me, helping me "take care of Snowball" as he chattered. He was a dear child, but his eager questions kept me busy. One advantage, though. He forced me to speak the white man's tongue – even more than I would have liked.

*****

It was the Moon-of-Ripening-Serviceberries when I felt I could wait no longer. I had to return to the Yampa band. I could hear them shouting and laughing across the shallow river at the racetrack. I shook my head at John when he tagged along.

"No, John," I told him. "I go home now. You stay."

"But I help you across the river! Snowball needs me!" he argued.

"No. You stay. I take Snowball." I spoke firmly.

And I was as firm with the terrified foal. I took his tether rope and led him quickly through the clear water that flowed around his ankles. He resisted, but I didn't stop.

And suddenly I was home again! I was in the midst of the Utes, milling about the racetrack. They stared at me in surprise. I looked for Moonlight and spotted her immediately. She raised her head high and whinnied. She recognized my scent.

I headed for her, with Snowball trotting at my heels. She looked a bit shabby, I thought critically. But she was fat and shiny, really. I pushed through the crowd, not pausing to greet my old friends.

All at once I was caught in great strong arms, arms that hugged me hard and let me go. It was Thunder Cloud! His face was beaming.

"Flying Horse! Come and run the next race! My last bet lost."

Like that. Just as though I had never been gone. He was in a good mood.

"Here. Follow me."

I followed. All at once we were with Storm. He looked from me to Thunder Cloud, something like fear in his eyes, I thought.

My father didn't stop to choose sweet words. He spoke quickly.

"Storm, my friend. I buy Moonlight now, as I told you. Five ponies. You choose. No bargaining."

For a minute I thought Storm would argue. And then I could see behind his eyes the uneasiness. The fear. And he knew a good deal when he saw it. This was a good deal. He nodded.

"Now?"

"Now. You choose your ponies later. Flying Horse will ride Moonlight in the next race."

It was as easy as that. No wasted words. No scolding. No asking for forgiveness. Nothing mattered but the race ahead.

At that moment I <u>was</u> Flying Horse again! I ran to Moonlight and put my cheek against hers. Quickly I gave her velvet nose a kiss and then jumped on her back. She turned and nuzzled Snowball a little, as though to see if he really was her own colt. She seemed satisfied.

"Thunder Cloud, hold Snowball while we race. I don't want him in the way."

The other riders lined up behind the starting rope. And we were off! I won. I knew I would. Moonlight and I were together again!

Chapter 6

Soon it was the Moon-of-Yellow-Leaves, and the aspen trees were like pools of sunshine on the mountains. It was my favorite moon, I think. It was the time when we women had finished making jerky and pemmican, and our men ceased their long hunting expeditions into the high country. And sometimes it was the season of stormy skies. That was when we got ready to get back to the White River country and sometimes even further. Sometimes we went on to the Grand River and to the great Grand Mesa beyond.

We didn't want to get caught in an early snow up here in the Yampa Valley. Early snows could be deadly; so hurriedly we broke camp, loaded on to our travois, rounded up our fat ponies, and headed for down river. My life with the family continued on just as before. It was as though I had never been gone.

The trip back seemed just half as long as the trip up. I wondered why. Before I could quite realize it, we were back in the White River country. I recognized familiar sights. We were at the Agency.

Thunder Cloud, always impatient to be on the way, had led the trek West. But now that we were here — _were_ we here?

I pulled up short. Where was the Agency? Had I lost my bearings? I turned and stared around in stupid confusion. The hills were the same. Dry and arid. The sagebrush flats were the same. But where the Agency buildings had stood were only some rough holes and a few piles of rock. What in the name of the Great Spirit had happened?

Thunder Cloud rode up beside me. We both stared. We had no words, only a fearful kind of daze. Had bad spirits turned the world upside down? Were evil spirits haunting us? Our legends told us of such strange things happening, of Little People who hid in the bushes and trees and shot invisible arrows at people. Were we being haunted by the Little People?

We turned and stared at each other, frightened. How could the entire Agency disappear? Even the Little People? How could they destroy all those buildings? They had not burned. There was no ash. No blackened traces.

Thunder Cloud rode around the spot where the buildings had stood, staring down at the Earth. He began to follow a kind of trail, where the weeds had been beaten into the ground by many feet. A long time he rode, his eyes on the Earth and I following. Then he stopped.

"Flying Horse," he turned to me, "you have good eyes for a trail. Follow it. I will go back. I get the others. I get our ponies. We follow you."

I rode and rode and rode, my eyes glued to the faint trail in the dry Earth. And as I rode, I couldn't get my mind off the Little People who might be haunting me, following along as I rode. I could feel it. I could feel the strangeness in the air. The harmony I had always felt with the Earth was suddenly gone. I felt lost and terrified. But I continued to ride.

I was riding into the wild brilliance of the sunset before I stopped. There was the White River, running smooth and serene beneath the sky when I saw them. The lights of the Agency in the distance! The people of the Agency lived! The Little People had not destroyed them!

The night was black before we finally reached the Agency. The buildings were the same. But they had just been moved a long day's ride down river. I sat on Moonlight while Lone Eagle and Little Bear rode up with Thunder Cloud.

He leaped off his horse and pounded on the door of the new Agent. I could see that he was very angry.

A strange elderly white man came to the door.

"What this mean?" shouted Thunder Cloud, indicating the entire areas with a wide gesture.

"What is your problem?" The Agent's voice was icy, like the cutting edge of a piece of river ice. "I am Father Meeker. And who are you? Please introduce yourself properly."

My father had lived with a white family in Utah for a while, when he was a child. He understood the white man's tongue. But understanding it didn't soothe his anger now.

"Why you move Agency?"

"Who are you?" The new Agent tried to freeze Thunder Cloud with a withering stare.

"Why?" Thunder Cloud roared again. "Why? Why move?"

The Agent started to close the door in my father's face. "Come back tomorrow." Thunder Cloud slammed the closing door against the Agent and held it open with his foot.

"No! Now! Tell me why move?"

All at once I realized the cause of my father's terrible anger. This new Agency stood in the middle of the old Ute racetrack — the wide fields where we had raced and grazed our ponies for generations. It was sacred ground for us.

They glared at each other, neither wavering. The scorn and obvious attitude of superiority in Mr. Meeker's face were intimidating, to say the least. But no one intimidated my father. He was accustomed to being heard.

"Why move?" he repeated one more time, holding the door open.

"I needed more land for my work."

"Your work?" Thunder Cloud snorted. "What work you do?"

"I'm going to teach you heathens how to farm. To work! To earn your lazy way in this world! Before I'm through with you, I'll make real men of you! Men of God! If you refuse to work, I'll refuse to issue you any government rations! Those who won't work won't eat! As simple as that!"

"But you plant Agency in Utes' pony pasture!" Father shouted.

"No more it's not! Next spring you plant crops here. You learn to farm!"

Thunder Cloud whirled away from the cold stare of the arrogant white man. He leapt on his pony and came back to where we were waiting in the darkness. He was too angry to talk. We pitched our camp that night in the pony pasture nearby.

*****

Next morning, early, a group of Utes gathered in front of our tipi. They were the ones who had remained at the Agency all summer, most of them. One was Quinket, a Yampa Ute who had come back early from the high country for some reason. He was an elder chief, but so quiet that we rarely heard his voice.

I could hear the anger in the voices of the group as they sat cross-legged in the early morning sunshine at the opening of our tipi.

"I told Old Nick that the site of the old agency was set by treaty," said Nicaagat, a young White River chief. "It couldn't be moved."

"Now who is Old Nick?" interrupted Thunder Cloud.

"That's what we call Agent Meeker. He insists we call him <u>Father</u> Meeker, so we call him Old Nick just to get his goat. Old Nick means the devil in white man's tongue."

"A good name for him!" muttered Thunder Cloud. "Old Nick."

"He's far worse than the other Agent!" went on Nicaagat. "He calls us savages. He thinks that his white God put him on this good green Earth just to remake us into his crazy ideas. He calls himself a missionary, whatever that is."

"He thinks he is going to make us over into farmers," old Quinket spoke up. "Farmers!" He almost spit the word on the dirt in front of him. "I tried to tell him that the Utes would never be farmers. That would be degrading to us. Farmers are only women! Or maybe slaves! We do not farm! We hunt! We are hunters. And warriors, when necessary. We will never dig up Mother Earth!"

That was the most I had ever heard old Quinket say in my life. I could tell he was very upset.

"He is trying to destroy everything we love in life!" went on Nicaagat, passionately. "He hates our ponies! He hates our racing! He hates our hunting! He says we are lazy and shiftless! He will soon remake us into his own pattern. May the Great Spirit save us!"

"Yes," spoke up Chief Colorow, another Ute who had come to our little powwow. We didn't know him well, for he was Chief of the Muaches, a band of Utes from the South of the Shining Mountains. The Great Father in Washington had earlier moved the Muaches from their home.

As they lived so far from the Agency, where government supplies were to be issued each month, the entire Muache band had been unceremoniously moved to a reservation just East of Denver. Chief Colorow, usually so easy-going, at first enjoyed Denver immensely. He and his band spent much of their time between supply issuances strolling the streets of this strange white man's town, staring into the shop windows, and howling with mirth over the strange things they found there. Utes love to laugh.

But then suddenly, without warning, they were moved to the White River Reservation, to be dumped into a strange band of Utes and crowded into an area already overloaded with inhabitants. The hunting was getting scarce, not the plentiful wild herds of olden days. Everyone resented this move.

Treaties meant nothing. Promises were only lies, as far as the Great Father in Washington was concerned. Hostility was building up in the usually friendly Ute people. I had already heard enough to know, even though I was young, that life for the Utes was becoming dangerous.

Occasionally I lifted my eyes to Lone Eagle, who sat in our tipi just across from me. He nodded his head often in agreement to what was being said just outside. And as often, he shook his head sadly at what he heard.

"When Old Nick moved the Agency down here to our pony pasture many of us refused to move," Chief Colorow was saying. "But he told us that if we didn't move down here, he would have the soldiers come in and move us by force. So we move. May the Great Spirit save us from the soldiers! Remember the Sand Creek Massacre!"

I could see Lone Eagle shiver at just the mention of that ghastly affair. I, too, felt the chill up my spine, remembering the grisly butchering of women, children and many old people by the troop of United States soldiers. I felt sick, just remembering.

I looked at Little Bear, sitting placid and silent beside Lone Eagle. She had turned off the conversation outside, turned off listening to things she didn't want to hear. She had her own ways of coping with things that might shake her sunny nature. I remembered Lone Eagle calling her his "happy Little Bear" in the old days. She was often singing, shutting out things she didn't like.

I shuddered, thinking of future possibilities. Thinking of soldiers marching into the White River Reservation, and what they might do to my beloved old grandparents. I was sick. Sick.

But Little Bear only smiled at me and started humming a little cradlesong.

Chapter 7

We settled into an uneasy season of sparse snows. We could see that the Great Spirit was unhappy with us. Usually He allowed us deep bands of snow each winter to be sure we had green pastures for our ponies the next year. And every time it snowed, we gave Him our loving thanks. It was a ritual with us.

Old Nick didn't help any. All that winter he kept preaching at us, nagging us for everything we did. We knew that he hated Indians. His lip curled with distaste every time he talked to one of us.

The first thing he did was to rename us all. He didn't like our Ute names. Said they were insane. Ugly. So I became Molly. Nicaagat was renamed Jack. Old Quinket was Douglas. And Canalla, our much-admired medicine man, was to be called Johnson.

He only renamed the ones with whom he came in frequent contact. I think he was afraid to give Thunder Cloud a new name. He probably felt that Thunder Cloud was very fitting.

He soon knew me, because I enrolled in Josie's little school. He tried to force all the Ute children on the Reservation to attend, but they always ran away and hid out somewhere whenever he went after them. He gave up on that idea.

Josie was Old Nick's daughter, and he wanted her to teach for more reasons than one, we soon heard. The Government paid her a good salary, as much as Meeker himself made. He liked that. But I really loved Josie. She was as different from Nick as day is from night. She was warm and laughing, nothing like the hateful Meeker or his witch of a wife, Arvilla. We called her a witch because she looked as though she was ready to quarter and cook one of us for dinner.

I was older than any of the children in Josie's classes, but I longed to learn everything there was on this wonderful Earth to learn. In spite of my loneliness during the past summer, I soaked up the white man's way of speaking, like thirsty ground soaks up rain.

Meeker soon learned that I understood almost everything he said, so he soon gave me odd jobs to do in his office. I hated that, as I hated him. But it was the price I had to pay for going to Josie's school.

"Mollie! Come here!" was heard often from his office.

I hated it. I hated being pulled out of Josie's happy class at his every whim. But I obeyed. It was easier that way.

Being there had one advantage, I soon found. I learned things about what was going on with other Utes. Sometimes things I heard I would rather have not heard. Old Nick was always plotting, planning in every way to destroy our way of life. He spoke of the Utes with scorn and disgust in his voice. I soon came to loathe him.

Long before anyone else at the Agency knew it, I knew of his plan to plow up our racetrack where we raced every Sunday. Before he came, we raced more often than that, every day that the weather was right and when we had plenty of venison on hand and no need to hunt. Our horses and our racing with them was our greatest joy in this great beautiful world that the Holy Spirit had created. Daily we gave thanks to Him as the sun rose clear and brilliant over the Shining Mountains.

As the heavy white furs of winter snow piled up to bury the dark evergreen trees along the White River, I laughed in Josie's schoolroom and carried notes or messages to others around the Agency. I was busy, but not too busy to keep an eye out for Morning Star. I had only brief glimpses of him occasionally.

Morning Star was becoming well known as a hunter. He was of the best hunters among the White River Utes. He preferred hunting to racing, I soon observed, perhaps because of his shy, quiet nature. He harkened to the silences of the mountains more than he did to the joyous shouts of the racetrack.

As Meeker worked on his plans to "civilize" the "stupid" Utes, he chose Quinket as his partner in the project. He had decided that the quiet, old man was the most amiable of the band. Quinket was also highly honored by his tribe because of his wealth (in ponies, as he owned more than a hundred) and for his wisdom.

And so I was often being sent with a message to "Douglas," as Meeker called him.

"Who?" I enjoyed pretending I didn't know who he meant. "Who did you say?"

"Douglas!" he would shout, vastly irritated. "You know...! The old man with all the horses!"

"Oh, you mean Quinket!" I would respond with sweet innocence. It was a game I always repeated and dearly loved.

But another thing Meeker didn't know, and that I wouldn't tell him, was that Quinket, in spite of his quiet, friendly ways, had lost most of his following among the young men to Nicaagat. The young Utes discovered that Nicaagat understood the underhanded way of white man better than anyone else at the White River Agency.

He was half-blood Apache and had lived with a Mormon family in Utah while he was a child. He had learned that white men often said one thing when they meant something else. He knew they often made promises that they had no intention of keeping. This was not a Ute's way. A Ute's promise meant forever — as long as the sun was in the sky and the Earth was under his feet.

Nicaagat had also worked with the whites as a scout for General Crook during the war with the Sioux tribe, so he was very familiar with their ways. He was also a good friend of Chief Ouray, the head of all the Ute tribes. Nicaagat had traveled to Washington on the Iron Horse with Ouray ten years earlier, when the Great White Father had asked them to come and sign another treaty.

When Meeker had first come to White River, Nicaagat was wearing his scout uniforms — frontier buckskins, Army boots, and a wide-brimmed military hat. He was also wearing his silver medal that the Great Father had given to all the Utes who had signed the treaty.

But it didn't help much. Meeker was not impressed. In fact, Meeker was more awed by Nicaagat's fierce manner. I think he was really afraid of him. But he soon realized that this warrior was a very important part of Ute life on the White River. And so I took frequent messages to him, too.

"Here, Mollie!" he would call out curtly. "Give Jack this message for me!"

"Jack?" I would smile at him. "Who is Jack?"

"Jack! Jack!" he would shout. "For God's sake! Jack! The Ute with the silver medal! Jack!"

"Oh, you mean Nicaagat!" And I would smile and bob my head a little. "I am sorry." I'm afraid I was learning a bit of the white man's deceptive way. And it was fun. I loved to see Meeker squirm.

One day, when the snow banks were deeper than usual beside the paths around the Agency, I went to Nicaagat's tipi and told him Old Nick wanted to see him.

"What does he want?" he growled. He was toasting a piece of jerky on the smoldering fire in the center of his tipi.

"I don't know. But he said to come right away."

Together we walked down to the Agency. Meeker was sitting behind his desk. Nicaagat stood silently, looking as fierce as usual.

"I want you to get some of the others and go out into the hills and chop a load of cedar fence posts. Bring them in and pile them up behind the Agency. Cut two or three hundred, at least."

"It's too cold. It's going to snow. We go on a sunny day."

"No! You go now! Today!"

"Why today? What you do with cedar posts?"

"That's my business. Do as I say, or you get no supplies when the government sends in our quota."

Silently the Ute stood before Meeker's desk, eyeing him coldly. They glared at each other for a time, neither blinking.

"What you do with cedar posts?" Nicaagat repeated.

Meeker saw he would get nowhere without a bit of explanation.

"When the ground thaws, you fellows will dig post holes out behind and build a big corral for your cows."

"Not for _my_ cows! I have no cows!"

"You will have! As soon as the corral is finished."

"We have no need of cows! We don't like cows! Why cows?"

"You are going to raise cows."

"Utes have no need for cows!" Nicaagat spoke with great authority. "No need for milk! This pasture for Ute ponies!"

"Who the hell says so?" The white man grew livid, the color of stale liver. I thought he might die, there in front of us.

"The treaty say so!"

"The treaty be damned! This land belongs to the Government! You lazy louts are only living here free, not even paying for it!"

Nicaagat pointed to the Earth beneath his feet with quiet emphasis.

"Treaty say this land is Ute land! I sign treaty in Washington!"

"Wait until I call in the soldiers! Then argue with _them_!"

The other turned a little pale, I thought. He had seen what the soldiers did to Indians – to Indian women and children, and to old people. I had heard what they did, and it now turned me sick, just thinking of Little Bear and Lone Eagle. But Nicaagat had _seen_ them doing it! He too looked sick.

"You call soldiers, that mean war," he said quietly. He turned on his heel and walked out of the Agency. Quickly I went back to Josie's schoolroom. I wish I could have stayed there.

So much for "Jack" and the fence posts.

But I knew that wasn't the end of it. Great rolls of barbed wire were lined up behind the Agency, and Meeker would get his fence built some way, I felt sure. His was an evil spirit. He never gave up.

A kind of rage pounded in my head, as I knew it did in the heads of the other Utes. The treaty with Washington said this was our land, forever and ever, I knew. Already the whites had taken away most of our land, leaving us only the Reservation. That was why they were to pay us in rations every month. And yet Old Nick didn't even allow us to have what we were promised. He was a devil! I hated him!

C h a p t e r   8

It was a balmy warm day in early spring when Old Nick gave me a call. It was a day when everyone on the Earth wanted to rejoice and celebrate all that the Great Father Sun had given us. I felt it. And I'm sure everyone in the schoolroom felt it, too. The small children looked at me in envy, as I went out into the golden sunshine.

"All right," Josie laughed. "The first day of real spring, so I'll give you all a spring vacation! Just go on out and play!"

They all stared at her in disbelief and sat speechless but not for long. She didn't have to tell them twice that they were free to leave.

"I'll see you in the morning!" she called after them.

"Go get Johnson!" growled Old Man Meeker. "And tell him to come immediately." He was running out of Utes he could order around.

He was in a bad mood. But I couldn't resist my little game with him.

"Who is Johnson? I don't know any Johnson," I asked softly.

"Johnson! Johnson!" he bellowed at me. "Get Johnson! Now!"

"But I don't know any Johnson," I asked with as much sincerity as I could manage without laughing out loud.

"Johnson! You know Johnson! The Medicine Man!"

I smiled as sweetly as I could.

"Oh, you must mean Canalla! Canalla, the Medicine Man! You mean the one who is the brother-in-law of Ouray, our Uncompahgre Chief?" I was feeling pretty good at really irritating him.

"Yes, yes, yes! Go!"

Why couldn't he call us by our own names? Canalla? That wasn't hard to say. He wanted to make all of us into white people. How long would it take him to learn it couldn't be done?

Canalla wasn't in his tipi. Of course not, who would be on a beautiful spring day? I turned and gazed around me in all directions, hoping to spy him. There he was, a quarter of a mile across the pony pasture. He was bent down, touching the Earth. I knew he was testing the soil, wondering how soon we could start racing. For years he had been in charge of the racing field.

My heart leapt. How soon would it be? I hadn't been on Moonlight all winter. How I longed to ride! As though spreading my wings, I began running across the field with wild abandon. For a moment, I forgot that I was a young woman of marriageable age and that I should behave as one. But even when I remembered, I didn't stop running. It was such joy. It was great to be young on a day in spring.

By the time I reached Canalla, I was panting.

"Old Nick!" I puffed. "Wants you! Now!"

Canalla was alarmed.

"Why? What the matter?" He started for the Agency, half trotting.

Then I laughed. He thought it was some terrible emergency.

"You needn't run," I laughed again. "I run only because it's spring! Wonderful spring! You can walk, though." Then I laughed again. "But fast! He's angry."

"That is not news!" He laughed, too.

Suddenly I really looked at him; really saw him as for the first time. And I had to howl with laughter. He looked so funny. I couldn't help it. He looked as he always looked, but in the strange tall silk hat, a plug hat, the other Utes called it, I thought, what a crazy way for a Ute to dress! He'd bought it in Denver some years ago and had worn it since. It was getting a bit shabby and tipsy. It was not a bright shiny black as it had once been, but it was a part of Canalla. It had never looked funny before today. I guess I had spring fever.

When we got back to Meeker's office, Josie was reading a newspaper aloud, her father sitting on the edge of his desk listening intently, a look of entranced pleasure on his face.

"First we will take away their hundreds of ponies," Josie read, "so they cannot roam and hunt, replace the ponies with a few draft horses for plowing and hauling, and then as soon as the Utes are thus forced to abandon the hunt and remain near the Agency, I will issue no more rations to those who will not work. I shall cut every Indian down to the bare starvation point."

Josie had finished the letter. She sat silent.

"Well?" Meeker asked her. "What do you think Senator Teller will say to that when he reads it?"

Canalla and I stood in the open doorway, silent. I was embarrassed, for I had understood every word of the letter. How much of it Canalla understood, I didn't know. It was a terrible letter. I was frozen with horror at the implications in it.

"Well," Josie said thoughtfully, frowning. "It's certainly not a letter I would write. I don't think this would be any solution for you, Papa. But knowing how Senator Teller hates the Utes, and how eager he is to get them shipped off to Indian Territory in Oklahoma, I think he'll like it. But don't ask me! You know I like the Utes!" She jumped up from the desk. Then suddenly she spied us.

"Oh, come in, Canalla!" she cried out, as embarrassed as I was at having overheard this overwhelming revelation. "I think Papa wants to see you."

"Yes, Miss," he said, bowing his head. "I am here."

"Yes, Johnson, I have some things to discuss with you. The rest of you can leave now."

No one ever knew just what went on at the confab, but one thing was certain. It was not good. Canalla was in a fury, but he would not discuss it. And for Canalla to be angry was most unusual. Everyone at the Agency was very fond of the Medicine Man and trusted his wisdom. He had always been considered one of the Utes most friendly with the white man.

I had learned that before old Meeker had come to the Shining Mountains as our new agent, he had been a writer for a newspaper in a far-off city called New York. He was always writing to people, to the Great Big Indian Agent in Washington, to the Governor of Colorado, to the Senator, like the letter we had overheard. And he liked to write to newspapers, those unfriendly to the Utes. He liked especially to see his name in print. It made him feel important, I think.

I learned a lot about him the more I was around him. He believed that all Utes were stupid and comprehended nothing that was said, so he talked quite freely with Arvilla and Josie in my presence. And, unhappily for me, I was understanding the white man's tongue much more often than I liked. And I didn't like what I heard.

One day, right after the mail pouch was delivered from Rawlins, he called his wife and Josie into his office to listen to his story in the Denver newspaper called the *Denver Tribune*. "Listen to this, ladies!" he said with considerable pride as he read.

The Utes are actual, practical Communists and the government should be ashamed to foster and encourage them in their idleness and wanton waste of property.

Living off the bounty of a paternal but idiotic Indian Bureau, they actually become too lazy to draw their rations in the regular way but insist in taking what they want wherever they find it. Removed to Indian Territory, the Utes could be fed and clothed for about one-half what it now costs the government.

Honorable N.C. Meeker, the well-known Superintendent of the White River Agency, was formerly a fast friend and ardent admirer of the Indians. He went to the Agency with the firm belief that he could manage the Indians successfully by kind treatment, patient precept and good example. But utter failure marked his efforts and at last he reluctantly accepted the truth of the border truism that the only good Indians are dead Indians.

I will admit that I didn't understand all of it. But those last words he read were a swift arrow straight in my heart. Dizzy and sick, I slipped out the open door and ran as fast as my moccasins could carry me, straight to our tipi. I was crying. I couldn't help it. I threw myself on my buffalo robe and wept.

Suddenly Little Bear was patting me gently on the shoulder.

"Little One, Little One," she whispered. "What troubles you?" She hadn't heard me cry since I was a baby. I never cried.

"That wicked man!" I tried to stifle my sobs.

"Who?" she asked. But I'm sure she knew. Everyone at the White River Agency knew. They didn't know all the facts that I did, but they knew.

"Old Nick! He wants us all dead! He says so!"

Little Bear would not listen to bad things said about anyone. She petted my head as she used to when I was little.

"Don't weep, Little One," she tried to soothe me. "You do not understand the white man's tongue."

"He wants to send us all to Indian Territory! Out on the plains where all Indians die in the heat! It is a sick land! He cannot send us there!"

Even the Utes, here in the safe sanctuary of our Shining Mountains, had heard of the devastating tragedy of all the Indian tribes that had been sent off to the virtual imprisonment of life in Indian Territory. They had died like flies. Only horror was to be found in Indian Territory. But there was no point in talking with Little Bear. She would only croon and comfort me.

But I must tell someone, someone who could stop him. That evening, when Lone Eagle came into the tipi, I crept close to him and whispered my terrified story.

"Please stop him!" I begged. "Please tell someone who can stop him!"

"Tomorrow, Little One," he replied in a comforting tone. But I could hear the anxiety in his voice, too. He believed me. "Tomorrow I tell the others."

But tomorrow was another day, another day of Big Trouble at the Agency. But this was a different kind of trouble.

Meeker shouted for me early in the day. Josie's classes had hardly started yet.

He always shouted. He thought that a Ute couldn't understand him unless he shouted.

"Mollie! Come here!" I was terrified, but I responded to his call instantly. I was expecting something. I didn't know what. "Bring me Johnson! And hurry!"

Today I didn't have the courage to play my little game with him. I wanted only to get away from him as quickly as possible. Of course he knew I knew he wanted Canalla. I walked the long walk to the far end of the large tipi village below the Agency buildings.

I didn't need sharp eyes to spot Canalla's plug hat as he sat before his tipi, basking in the sun, while his several wives knelt nearby, working over a large elk skin. All Ute women were skilled at tanning the hides of the game their hunter husbands brought home. But Canalla wasn't much of a hunter, for he was often too busy with his duties as Medicine Man or as the boss man of the pony races, which took a good deal of time during the racing season. The skin was a gift, probably.

He looked up as I approached. He shook his head sadly, guessing at my message.

"Old Nick again?"

"Yes. And he says to hurry."

"He always say hurry." Wearily he got to his feet and followed me back through the village where other Ute wives were busy scraping deer and elk skins. Today was a perfect day for tanning, and the whole village was busy.

Everyone looked up and greeted Canalla as we passed. He was much loved among the Utes, I knew.

"Good morning, Johnson!" exclaimed Meeker as we came in. He was actually smiling as he held out his hand to shake. "Sit down! Sit down!"

What had come over the man? This wasn't the Meeker I knew. He was speaking with a wicked tongue this time for sure. I busied myself around the office, picking up letters scattered about and piling them neatly upon the corner of the big desk. I was bursting with curiosity.

"Johnson!" He got immediately to the point, smiling benignly. "Please forgive me for speaking as I did the other day. I know it upset you, and I am truly sorry."

Canalla lowered his head, making no response. His face was expressionless.

"I've decided to make amends. I am going to build you a house!"

The other looked up in surprise.

"A house?"

"Yes, a house. A white man's house!"

"Like Chief Ouray's house at Los Piños Agency?' He was clearly astonished. Meeker nodded.

"Why? I have a good tipi," Canalla persisted.

"Yes, but you have many wives. You need more room."

"Why you say this? Why you make me a house?"

"Frankly, I need your help. You are an important man here. What do you say?"

Canalla slowly shook his head.

"I have tipi. Utes like tipi. Utes no like corners. We like houses round. No place for bad spirits." He turned and walked from the room.

But before the day was done, "Johnson's" house was going up, just across the way from the Agency. The sawing and the hammering shattered the silence of the very mountains. We hated this racket made by the white workmen that Meeker had imported to "civilize" us. Hideous!

Chapter 9

And then it was the Moon-of-the-Awakening-Bear. If the warmth of the season had not awakened him this year, the white carpenter and his assistant would surely have done it with their hellish pounding. Canalla's house was growing fast.

The Bear Dance came, but it didn't feel like a celebration of joy this year. The White River band built the usual round dance corral out in the middle of the racetrack with many of the Yampa Utes assisting in bringing in the logs and brush. The opening faced the East, as always, welcoming the spring sun.

Men from the hunting parties were bringing in fresh game for the big barbeque that was to follow. We should have been excited, but we weren't. The sky seemed dark, in spite of the sunshine.

Thunder Cloud came into our tipi late the night before the dance. His voice was quiet, but it seemed that he shouted his announcement.

"We do not go up to the Shining Mountains this year." His words hung heavy in the air.

"Why, Papa?" I knew, but I had to ask.

"The White River Utes need me. There is blood on the wind."

"You are wise, my Son," was Lone Eagle's response. "We may all be needed before this summer is over."

The Bear Dance went on as usual. I was happy to see that Morning Star was there. With the first rasping of the "bear-claw" musician, I invited him to dance. I was so afraid that someone else would invite him. We were the first dancers in the center of the dance corral. This time he smiled at me, his wide generous smile. And I could see the warmth in his eyes. I had some trouble trying to conceal my joy. He did like me!

We danced for three days. Meeker had told our chiefs, "Jack" and "Douglas" and "Johnson," that he didn't approve of wasting valuable time in such nonsensical activities, but no one listened to him. While we danced, the white carpenters worked on Canalla's house. The din was ear splitting.

The day after the Bear Dance, a few of the Yampa Utes struck their tipis and set out for the Shining Mountains. I hated to see them go without us, but deep inside, I was glad I would remain near Morning Star.

Josie went on with her school as usual, although I was often the only one there, except for little May Price, the four-year-old daughter of Flora Ellen Price. Shadrach Price was Meeker's plowman. Flora Ellen helped the Meeker women in the kitchen. She kept little two-year-old Johnnie with her.

All the Utes at White River adored the beautiful little towheaded children and persisted in trying to buy them in exchange for some of their best racing ponies. But Flora Ellen ignored the high bidding. She was happy as she was.

I was also amused at a young White River Ute, Persune, who often came to Josie's classes. He was even older than I, so at first I couldn't imagine why he, out of all the Utes, was so interested in getting an education. But it didn't take me long to understand. He was passionately in love with Josie. I think most of the young Utes were, but they didn't approach their love affair in the same way. Every day, after school, Persune stayed and asked her to marry him. She always laughed off his serious proposals, but he didn't lose interest. He was one of her most faithful students and was learning English quite well, even though it was not his main interest.

Shortly after the Yampas had left for the High Country, we had our first pony races. Because of such a winter drought, we were able to begin races earlier than usual. Canalla announced that the Earth had dried enough for a race on Sunday. Sunday, or any day in the week, had meant nothing to us before Meeker came. Days were simply days. They had no names and no significance to us.

But Old Nick had forbidden any racing except on Sunday, so it was Canalla's task to figure out when Sunday was and to have races only on that day. His announcement was met with great pleasure. The crowd had already gathered at the racetrack before we had the ponies rounded up. They couldn't wait to start the racing – and the betting.

Betting was the most popular game that we ever played. Winter or summer, we loved betting on anything and everything. But betting on the horses was the best.

I would race on Moonlight, of course. I was the only woman to race, ever. Little Bear and Lone Eagle sternly disapproved, but Thunder Cloud had spoiled me from earliest childhood, and he was proud of my winning. He knew he had a winning combination in Moonlight and me. We usually won, and he was as delighted with my success as if I had been the son he had always wanted.

But this year, I was conscious of Morning Star's eyes on me as I lined up with the ponies in the opening race. Suddenly I was ashamed. My face burned red, I knew. What would he think of me? Would he think me unfit as a woman? Would he not want me as a wife? I wanted to drop out of the race now, before it started, but my pride and sense of honor kept me in line. The bets were already set on this first race, I knew. I couldn't let my friends down or embarrass Thunder Cloud. He would be humiliated forever. I had to run.

I petted Moonlight's snowy neck to quiet her. The first race of the year was as exciting for our ponies as it was for us. They were flighty and hard to hold down. I crooned to her as I patted her smooth shoulders. She was prancing. Finally Canalla raised his arm with his pistol in hand.

"Ready?"

"Bang!" The gun rang out and the ponies were off. But my usual burst of excitement was blotted out by the shame I felt with Morning Star's eyes on me, following me accusingly around the track.

I tried to hold Moonlight back. I didn't want to win. That would only mean more attention from the spectators. But she jerked on her bridle and surged ahead. There was no holding her down. She was accustomed to winning. And she would win.

I could hear the crowd roaring as we circled around the far side of the track. And the pounding of the other ponies' feet were close behind me. There was no holding us back now. Moonlight's feet seemed to tear up the Earth in forging ahead.

I pulled hard on her halter rope, but it was no use. The other ponies closer, closer, drowning out the yelping of the excited Utes. And then it was over. We had won.

I rode over to the pasture, jumped from Moonlight's back, and jerked the rope from her head. I would never race again. Never. Young Snowball came galloping up to us, but I gave him a little swat on the rump and walked back to the cheering crowd, ashamed.

Morning Star was nowhere to be seen. He may have thought me a good pony racer, but not a good prospect for a wife. What had I done? Little Bear was right. I had ruined my life, as she had been warning me since I was a little girl.

I had planned to go back to our tipi and go to bed, "sick." That's what I would tell everyone. But then I saw Josie in the crowd. She was laughing and cheering and clapping her hands. She loved the racing as much as the Utes did.

"Flying Horse!" She ran out onto the racetrack and threw her arms around me. "You won! You won! Congratulations! And I won my bet on you!"

Her love and warm enthusiasm began to drive the black clouds into the back of my thinking and I decided to spend the rest of the day watching the races. But I was never going to race with the young men again. I was going to become a "suitable wife." I secretly prayed that Morning Star wouldn't scorn me forever.

Josie had a wonderful day and, as a result, I did, too. She was such great fun. She loved the Utes and they loved her. How could she be so different from her arrogant father?

*****

As the hot dry summer wore on, Meeker spent more and more time writing letters to the newspapers, to the governor, to the Indian Bureau in Washington, everywhere he could make himself heard.

He had a long list of complaints against the Indians, against all Indians but against the White River Utes in particular. We were lazy, shiftless, dangerous, treacherous, and uncooperative in every way.

"Mollie!" he bellowed one day. "Come here!" I went into his office. "Go get Johnson for me!"

"I'm sorry. Canalla not here. By Rawlins. Hunting buffalo."

He slapped the desk with an angry hand.

"When will he be back?"

How was I to know? When he got a buffalo, maybe? I stood silent.

"Go tell his family to have him see me the minute he returns."

I went out into the blazing sun and set off for the Medicine Man's tipi. There was no more sawing and pounding in the new house across the road. It must be finished. That was probably the reason Meeker wanted to see him. Why else?

I hated the roasting heat of this summer. Having spent every summer of my life in the Medicine Springs country and above, I was unaccustomed to this kind of weather. And even the White River Utes were suffering. Most of them were in the north, supposedly hunting for game but also seeking some relief from the dry burning sun.

And the heat didn't help Meeker's bad temper. Through the mail sack to Rawlins, he was building a heated campaign against the Utes, in partnership with Governor Frederick Pitkin and William B. Vickers, the editor of the *Denver Tribune*. A favorite headline for these three was "The Utes Must Go."

Pitkin was the tremendously rich gold miner who had been able to engineer the treaty that took the gold-rich San Juan Mountains away from the Utes and turned them over to the greedy white prospectors who came pouring into Colorado in a ravenous flood. As a result he was made the first governor when Colorado became a state in 1876.

Vickers had been Governor Pitkin's secretary before he decided to become a newspaper editor. He had Pitkin's whole-hearted cooperation in the newspaper business, so the two worked together like a hand in a glove. They both loathed all Indians. They burned with fanatical zeal to get the Utes moved to Indian Territory. "The Utes Must Go! rang across the state.

By terrible coincidence, even the weather played into their hands. Days and weeks and months without rain turned the Colorado mountains into dry tinder. Father Sky gave them lightning — but no rain. So numerous forest fires popped up across the entire state, from North to South. It didn't take Indian-haters long to grab this as a weapon in running out the Utes.

On the Fourth of July, while the whites in Denver were busy setting off fireworks to celebrate their breaking free from England little more than 100 years earlier, Vickers was busy preparing a telegram to send off to Washington. Addressed to the Commissioner of Indian Affairs, it read:

Reports reach me daily that a band of White River Utes are off their reservation, destroying forests.... They have burned millions of dollars of timber and are intimidating settlers and miners.... I am satisfied that there is an organized effort on the part of the Indians to destroy the timber of Colorado. These savages should be removed to Indian Territory where they can no longer destroy the forests of this state.

Vickers sent it off the next day, with the Governor's signature. Later in the week, I chanced to be in Meeker's office when he opened the Rawlins mail bag.

"Mollie!" Meeker thundered. "Run get Jack! And Douglas! And Johnson! Now!"

I was afraid of what was coming. Only that morning Nicaagat had asked me to translate a clipping from the Denver newspaper that a white friend named Peck had brought him. It said that the Utes had been setting fires along the Yampa River and had burned down the house of James B. Thompson, who used to be the Indian Agent here at White River. I couldn't believe this. Thompson had been a friend of the Utes.

But I hurried off. As I went toward the far end of the village of tipis, I saw a group of men crowded in front of Nicaagat's home. The trouble had already started.

The chief was speaking with evident anger, waving the piece of newspaper in his hand. There was a growling among the men. He interrupted himself as he saw me approach.

"Old Nick?" He knew my messages were from the Old Man himself.

I nodded. "He wants you. And Quinket. And Canalla. And fast!"

"Canalla hunting buffalo. Rawlins. But I no go. I go to Denver. I see the Governor! Mr. Peck take me. Now."

My heart twisted in my chest. No one ever refused Old Nick's message. Not until now

Chapter 10

Nicaagat and Peck set off on their ponies into the blazing mid-summer heat, off up toward the Shining Mountains, which they would have to cross on the way to Denver. It would be a long hard trip, so we knew they would be gone several days.

"Tell Old Nick I go to Thompson's house first. I see if Utes burn it. It is lie, I say."

We learned when he returned that it <u>was</u> a lie. The house was still standing firm and unburned beside the Yampa where he had built it some years ago. We also learned upon Nicaagat's return that upon his arrival the Governor had refused to see him. But he was determined. He sat outside Governor Pitkin's office day after day, awaiting his chance to slip through an open door. He told us the whole story.

"Governor much surprise. Ask how things go on White River. Say much in newspapers about Ute on White River. I say that why I here in Denver. He show me letter from Agent. I say no read, come Denver instead. I tell him letter is only lies. Thompson house not burn. Ute set no fires. Not anywhere. I tell him please write Washington. Tell Great Father send us new Agent. Utes want Meeker go home. No like Utes. He say yes. Next day he write Washington. But I think he lie. All white men lie. Speak with wicked tongue."

Back on White River, things were no better. Canalla came back from his hunting trip up in Rawlins country in an exuberant mood...for a time at least. He'd shot a great buffalo, which took three horses to pack it home. He'd taken two of his wives with him, to help butcher and skin it. But beneath the exuberance was a somber kind of sorrow.

"The last, I think," he said, showing us the huge head. "No more buffalo. None left for Utes. What for beds now? What for tipis?"

Ile turned and walked into his tipi, walking like a very tired, very old man. Then I remembered.

"Canalla!" I called out to him. "Old Nick say come now. Fast!"

After a time, he reappeared, the heavy lines on his face making him older than he was. He trudged slowly across the tipi village to the Agency. He went in. Anxious, we all waited, while there was only silence from the Agency building. A long, long while we waited. His three wives were silent, as we all were.

A brilliant red sunset was burning in the West before he finally came out, looking even older than when he went in. We waited, breathless, as he approached us.

"How?" Quinket greeted him.

Canalla shook his head.

"Not good."

"No?" We all held our breath, waiting.

"Meeker want my help."

"How? What help?"

Canalla shrugged, spreading his hands helplessly. How could he explain?

"He make me a house. A square house. I no like."

Quinket nodded wisely.

"No Utes like square corners. A place for bad Little People."

"Old Nick say he want me for a friend," said Canalla. "I no understand."

"He want you for his dirty work," was Quinket's response. And an accurate one, I felt sure. I felt very sorry for poor Canalla. Such a good man. A true friend of both Utes and of white men. He was in a bad place to be. Caught in the middle.

"So? What goes?" Quinket asked.

"Too tired to fight," the other answered, his shoulders sagging. "We move into square house tomorrow." He turned and walked into his tipi...for the last time. Our lives seemed to be ending at least the way we knew them.

The next day held more than the excitement of Canalla's move into the House-With-Square-Corners. There was a telegram in the mail pouch from Rawlins, directed to Meeker, Indian Agent. I heard him read it aloud to Arvilla and Josie. He read:

Governor of Colorado reports your Indians depradating near North and Middle Parks. If correct take active steps to secure their return to reservation. The secretary directs that if necessary you will call upon nearest military post for assistance.

"What good will that do?" thundered Meeker. "As you damned well know, I've written repeatedly to Major Thornburgh at Fort Steele and never got a peep in response! I've been asking him all summer to clean the Utes out of Yampa River Valley and out of Little Snake Valley! And I haven't yet heard a word from him!"

And then, to further fire Meeker's rage was a letter from Governor Pitkin, urging him to call in the troops to remove all Utes to Indian Territory, several hundred miles to the East. He called it Oklahoma. I listened as he read it aloud.

Suddenly I saw a curtain of fear drop over his face. He was afraid! Meeker! I felt a queer kind of pleasure in seeing it. I think he began to realize that the bonfire he had started was beginning to burn out of control.

"I must get to Denver immediately!" He sounded like he was choking on his own words. He was afraid for himself, afraid for his own life and for Arvilla and Josie.

What he didn't know was that the contents of the Governor's letter had reached the Ute chiefs, Nicaagat and Quinket, almost as soon as it had reached him.

Move all Utes to Indian Territory in the East, where Indians died like flies...? It was unthinkable!

*****

Meeker set out immediately for Denver, far across the Shining Mountains. It was a long, complicated journey. But he had word that General John Pope, a well-known general during the Civil War who was a good friend of Meeker, was in Denver. When Meeker was a war correspondent, he had made Pope even more famous than he deserved, thus winning a great lifetime friend. He could get General Pope's help with the Utes, he was sure.

As it turned out, Pope wasn't much help. When Meeker reported his failure to "civilize" the Utes, General Pope only smiled kindly and advised him to have patience. "Rome was not built in a day, you know."

But it was on the long trip back to White River that something occurred that would change Meeker's life forever.

When he boarded the Denver Pacific in Denver, headed for Cheyenne, he was trying to build up his courage. Pope had assured him that if he ever needed military help, he could call on the "Buffalo Soldiers," as Captain Dodge's Company D was popularly called. They were the forty-four black cavalrymen stationed at Pagosa Springs, so-called for their curly hair. And they were alerted to come immediately if Meeker called for help.

When Meeker changed trains at Cheyenne, taking the Union Pacific to Rawlins, a strikingly handsome young U.S. Army officer entered the "palace car" and took a seat near Meeker. Meeker struck up a conversation and discovered that this handsome young man was Major Thornburgh, a charming graduate of West Point. When the Agent introduced himself, Thornburgh recognized him immediately.

He explained he had been absent from Fort Steele for some weeks, entertaining Webb Hayes, the son of President Hayes. They had been on a prolonged hunting trip and had shot a magnificent buck. Thornburgh had just carried the head to Cheyenne to be mounted for young Hayes.

The conversation had been lively and friendly until Meeker began unloading his long list of prejudices against the faults of the military. Not known for his tact, he worked himself up to a frenzy of fury before they reached Rawlins. They parted with the bitterest of emotions on both sides.

At Rawlins, Meeker met Harry Dresser, a young white man from the Agency, who had come to pick up the Agent and a new employee he had hired, George Eaton. As they were driving home, the wagon upset as they were coming down toward Williams Fork. Meeker was caught under the wagon, and his left arm was seriously wrenched. The wagon was completely wrecked.

The two young men propped Meeker up against a rock and left him there all night while they came back to the Agency and got a new wagon. We should have been terribly sorry for the old man, but I'm afraid we couldn't scare up any sympathy for him. He hated every one of us with a passion, and we all knew it.

When he got back to the Agency and found that Nicaagat had just gotten back from his own trip to Denver to complain to Governor Pitkin, he was furious. He told "Jack" that he deserved to be hanged for his disloyalty. He also accused him of starting more forest fires on the Gore Range above Steamboat Springs as a way of getting even for Captain

Dodge's "Buffalo Soldiers" being stationed in Middle Park.

Everyone at White River seemed to be getting angrier each day. The weather may have had something to do with it. The burning heat of late summer was wearing on all of us, I know. We hadn't had a drop of rain since before the Bear Dance, and the horse pastures were burning up. We were beginning to be very worried about our poor ponies. They were finding it rough going to find enough to eat. And we Utes loved our ponies as much as our children.

It was early in the Moon-of-Turning-Leaves that the sheriff from Hot Sulphur Springs arrived at the Agency with a warrant for the arrest of two of our Utes, two that he called "Bennett" and "Chinaman." We all swore that they had never left the Reservation to set fire to James Thompson's barns, their supposed crime. But Meeker let the sheriff take them anyway, further infuriating us.

Everything at the Agency seemed to be at the point of explosion. Nerves were tight and ragged. Everyone snapped and snarled at everyone else.

The bursting point came early one morning when Old Nick shouted at me from the office.

"Mollie!" he bellowed. "Come here!"

I went running, terrified by his tone.

"Bring me Shadrach Price! Immediately! And don't dawdle!"

I never dawdled. I didn't know what it meant. So I raced around the Agency, seeking him.

The summer before, when Meeker had started out to try to teach us to become "human," he had sent word to the East to get some workmen to help him. Shadrach was the plowman he had gotten from Kansas to teach us to dig up our Mother Earth. He was a criminal in the Utes' eyes. To rip open our Mother's very bowels! We could imagine nothing more evil! A sin against her, as well as all the gods, and even a sin against Father Sun, to whom we prayed daily to forgive Shadrach Price.

And Shadrach had done nothing to redeem himself in the eyes of the Utes. His frequent bragging about his shooting nine Indians on the Plains East of Denver on his way West with Flora Ellen and the children infuriated them. He was especially proud of having scalped them, he repeated, scowling around at any Ute in the area. No one liked Shad Price. But he knew how to plow.

I finally located him, out behind the barn, mending some harness.

"Old Nick wants to see you! And he says to hurry!"

"No one tells me to hurry!" he growled. But I noticed that he got up quickly to go to the Agency office. No one wanted to antagonize Meeker. Not these days.

I could scarcely keep up, but I too rushed back to the office. I got there just in time to overhear Meeker's orders.

"Get your plow out there — now! And plow up that damned racetrack!"

Plow up the racetrack? I refused to believe it.

"We're going to plant winter wheat there next week!"

His words roared in my head. Plow up the racetrack! I couldn't believe my ears. Should I run and warn somebody? But who? I struggled with my own conscience until the men came in for the noon meal in the boarding house.

As I slipped into the dining room I heard one of the Greeley boys speaking.

"I'm not afraid for my life. No more than I would be in my mother's dooryard. But I don't blame the Utes for not wanting this area plowed up. It's a great place for the ponies. And there's lots better ground down near the river for planting."

"Yeah!" answered another. "And I heard Chief 'Douglas' telling him the other day that he'd have his band clear off the sagebrush so they could plow it up."

"But Meeker is a stubborn old cuss! He swears he'll plow up the race track or get the soldiers in here to <u>force</u> the Utes to do it!"

"Yep! It's going to be a toss-up to see how this thing is going to turn out!"

Everyone at the table laughed. Everyone but Shad Price. He looked like a thunderstorm.

"It's gonna be plowed!" he growled. "I'm tellin' ya!"

Chapter 11

That afternoon Shad Price hauled the plow out to the racetrack and began his first furrow. Almost immediately, half a dozen angry young Utes were walking along beside him, each carrying a loaded rifle. Their hot eyes were flashing anger.

"You stop now," they warned him. "Stop now and we no shoot."

Shad may have killed nine Plains Indians, but he was now unarmed. He unhitched his horses in mid-furrow and took the team to the barn. He then went into the Agency to report.

As the Greeley boys had said at dinner, Meeker was a "stubborn old cuss."

Furious, he sent Shad back to the barn to get his horses and resume the plowing. But this time, the angry young warriors didn't speak to Shad. They didn't even approach him. They shot warning shots over his head and around his feet. He needed no more notice of future action. Hurriedly he unhitched his team and set off for the barn at a lope.

Everyone around the Agency was watching from behind every bush and building. A wild cheer of approval broke out, shattering the silence.

Meeker was furious. He immediately wrote a letter to the Commissioner of Indian Affairs in Washington, so he could send it off in the mail pouch to Rawlins. Before he sealed the letter, he read it aloud to Arvilla, who was sitting nearby, reading her enormous book, *Pilgrims Progress*. I was studying nearby.

"This is a bad lot of Indians," he read. "They have had free rations for so long and have been flattered and petted so much that they think themselves lords of all."

"How was that?" he asked her, looking up for her approval, which he invariably got.

"Well written, dear," she reassured him.

He arose stiffly from his chair and took the letter to Wilson, the mail carrier. He hadn't been gone long when Canalla came in. Arvilla looked at the tall Medicine Man with sudden fear. His face was distorted with anger. Canalla, usually so calm and pleasant to everyone he met. Canalla, who was her husband's friend and ally, and Canalla, for whom her husband had built the house across the street, had never frightened her before.

"I want Meeker," he demanded bluntly.

"He just stepped out," was her hurried response as she got to her feet.

"I wait."

She went to Meeker's chair and fluffed up the cushions that she had arranged to ease his aching shoulder. He soon returned and sank uneasily into his chair. He seemed to ignore Canalla. But Canalla was not to be ignored.

He began shouting in a rushing mixture of Ute and English so fast that I couldn't understand more than an occasional word. Neither could Meeker. At last, he slowed down and spoke with great force.

"You plow up my pony track! You plow up my Earth! This land belong to Utes! It is written in treaty!"

"The land is not Ute land! It is government land! It is my land to do with as I see fit! I say it will be plowed!" Meeker shouted in return.

Again the Medicine Man broke out in a fury of Ute. But Meeker interrupted him, speaking slowly and distinctly.

"The trouble is this, Johnson. You have too many ponies. You had better kill some of them." I froze in my chair, sickened.

Canalla was suddenly silent. He stared at the other, totally dumbfounded. He couldn't conceive of such blasphemy. Slowly he walked around Meeker's big desk and picked up the withered old man by the shoulders. He hustled him across the room to the open door and out on to the porch. Arvilla ran screaming in pursuit.

Two white workers came to her aid just in time to see Canalla fling Meeker against the hitching rail with violence. He turned and walked silently to the House-With-the-Square-Corners and disappeared inside.

The workmen helped move the Agent from the hitching rail and back into his office. Meeker felt himself all over, then announced that he was not really hurt. Just shaken up.

"What hurts most," he said, "is to think after I built him a house at Agency expense, he would do this to me."

Meeker lay awake all night, he told Arvilla, pondering his next move. Next morning, he called Josie into his office and dictated letters to Governor Pitkin and Senator Teller. He also dictated a telegram to Commissioner Hayt in Washington. I heard him reading the telegram aloud to Arvilla.

> I have been assaulted by a leading chief, Johnson, forced out of my house and injured badly but was rescued by employees. It is now revealed that Johnson originated all the trouble stated in the letter Sept. 8. His son shot at plowman, and opposition to plowing is wide. Plowing stops. Life of self, family and employees not safe. Want protections immediately. Have asked Governor Pitkin to confer with General Pope.
>
> N.C. Meeker, Indian Agent

But even after getting her approval, he hesitated. Would he come out on top if he went ahead with his campaign of hate? He recalled his own words directed with such force at Major Thornburgh.

"Bringing in the military only makes matters worse where the Indians are involved!" he remembered shouting at the handsome young soldier, sitting so cool and self-assured in the "palace car" of the Union Pacific. "Just think back on the shameful slaughter you young military upstarts carried out in the Sand Creek Massacre not many years back!" he had gone on in an accusing voice.

And he remembered Thornburgh's response.

"Don't blame me! I was still in knee pants at that point!" was his lofty answer.

The telegram to Commissioner Hayt and the letters to Governor Pitkin and Senator Teller were still on his desk the next evening when John Steele, who owned the mail contract from Rawlins to White River, arrived. He was a most unhappy supper guest. He told Meeker that he'd been losing money on his mail contract since July because of the Ute problems. No one wanted to carry the mail into White River. Three of his riders had refused point blank to carry the mail for him.

"Too dangerous!" they said. He had only one left, Black Wilson, and he had been threatening to quit for the past couple of weeks. It had cost Steele a fortune greasing palms in Rawlins to keep things rolling. The redskins were about to put him out of business.

"What kind of government do we have in Washington if they can't protect their citizens?"

I was hiding behind the kitchen door when I saw Meeker get up from the table, go into his office and bring back the telegram and the two letters. He slit them open and handed them to Steele to read.

"Troops!" whooped the man from Rawlins. "Just what we need! Just what the doctor ordered! Now we'll get some action!" He was exuberant.

Meeker was delighted with this response.

"Can I mail them off for you?"

Meeker nodded.

"I'll be outa here by daylight in the morning!" crackled Steele like an old hen. "The War Department in Washington will have your telegram in four days!"

Four days! We had little time to prepare! I closed the kitchen door quietly and slipped out the back. I raced across the street to Canalla's House-With-Square-Corners as fast as my feet would fly. I pounded on his door.

Susan opened the door. She was Chief Ouray's sister and Canalla's favorite wife. She smiled until she saw the terror in my face.

"What is it? Come in! Come in!" She put her arm around me and closed the door.

"Canalla!" I choked. "Tell Canalla...!"

But the tall Medicine Man himself stood before me.

"What is your news?"

"Old Nick... He has asked for soldiers to come here! Four days! We have four days before they come!"

"This means war!" His voice was quiet but stern. "I tell Chief Nicaagat." He spoke as though he had been expecting such news.

Before morning every Ute at the Agency knew of Meeker's telegram to Washington. My mind was in a turmoil of images, horrible images. Manacles. Hand cuffs. Utes hanging by nooses from trees. Utes locked up for life in prisons. All the Utes in Colorado being herded off like cattle to that deadly Indian Territory in the East. Things Meeker had so often mentioned during the summer. I was sick.

"Mollie!" came Meeker's thundering call the next morning. Apparently he had been thinking over the possible results of his appeal for military help. And it scared him. "Run and get Jack! And hurry!"

"Nicaagat is not at the Agency today," I told him.

"How do you know?" He looked at me with an accusing glare.

"I don't know," I lied. "I only know he is not here."

Meeker looked stricken. He cast his eyes around his office, as though looking for a way out. I stood silent.

"Send him in! The minute he gets back!"

But the news had already spread like wildfire. Nicaagat had ridden up the Chief Quinket's village to have a conference of war, for that's what all the Utes were expecting. But Nicaagat wanted peace.

"I told Quinket," he said later. "We Utes have to stick together. If we are to live, we must forget any past differences between Yampa Utes and White River Utes. And he pledged us his cooperation."

All the young Utes were in a furor. All summer they had been hearing Meeker's threats of shackles and ropes and life imprisonment. They believed that the soldiers were coming to drag or drive them to the dreaded Indian Territory to take them away from their beloved Shining Mountains forever and to slaughter their ponies. They would never submit! Never! They would fight to the death.

Quinket agreed. But he also agreed with Nicaagat. He would strive for a peaceful solution.

I sent him in to see the Agent upon his return. Nicaagat told us about it later.

"I told Old Nick that the soldiers were coming and that I hoped he would stop them from coming to the Agency. He told me it was none of my business. I asked him to come with me to meet the soldiers and talk with them. He got mad and said I was all the time molesting him. He got up and went out of his office. He locked the door behind him. That was the last time I ever saw him."

Chapter 12

While we waited for the government troops to arrive, the hills around the Agency burned in all their glory. The aspens had turned to their richest gold, and the serviceberry bushes were as red as ripe strawberries. But no one saw the beauty of the mountains that year. Or if they did, they were too angry or too frightened to mention it.

The days dragged on. Five. Six. Seven. Meeker called me in.

"Mollie! Bring Jack to me. Immediately!"

"Jack. Sit down," he said when Nicaagat came in. This was an unheard of courtesy. He never asked Utes to sit down, not even chiefs, like Nicaagat. He was trying to be friendly, I suppose. "I'm sure you've heard how Johnson mistreated me."

"He didn't mean anything by that," the Chief laughed a little, as though at their own little joke. "It really wasn't anything to worry about. Forget it."

I marveled at his self-restraint. He was determined to make peace with this strange white man.

"I will <u>not</u> forget it!" Meeker shouted. "And I will complain about it!"

"It is very bad business to make a big rumpus over such a little thing," Nicaagat consoled him.

"It is not a little thing! And what's more, I'm going to see to it that the soldiers drive you Utes out of the State of Colorado!"

How could Nicaagat continue to sit quietly and listen to this fool? I longed to leap up and pound Old Nick in the face.

"But you cannot do this," the Chief said softly. "This land is our land. Utes live in this Land of Blue Sky many hundred years. Long before Columbus. Long before white man come."

I was astonished to hear Nicaagat speak with such knowledge. This Ute! Then I remembered. He once had lived for a time as a child with Mormons in Utah.

"Get out of my office!" Meeker shouted, pointing to the door.

*****

The hot autumn days dragged on. And still no soldiers. At last, Ute scouts came pounding up to the Agency in a great lather. Thornburgh's long line of troops had been sighted at Fortification Creek. It would probably be another four days before they reached the Agency. It was all the chiefs could do to restrain the young braves. They had overheard Meeker bragging that Thornburgh would have wagons loaded with handcuffs and shackles and ropes. Several bad Utes would be hanged and others taken as prisoners. And now they could actually see those loaded wagons.

"Let us kill the devils!" was the cry. But Nicaagat shook his head.

"We do not want to fight the soldiers," he repeated, over and over again. "We must be friends with the soldiers. They are our brothers, remember. We are all brothers. The two-leggeds, the four-leggeds, the winged ones and the rooted, we all have the same Mother Earth, the same Father Sun. We will not kill our own brothers. We must love them."

We had heard this a thousand times before. It was our religion. We had heard it from our elders since we were babies. We had heard it around the campfires on summer evenings. And we had heard it over the winter fires in our tipis at night.

But I don't think any of the young Utes wanted to hear it again. They were sick of hearing that we must "love" Old Nick. Even I, a girl, hated him with a passion. When he said, "You'd better kill your ponies," I had wanted to kill him myself. Please forgive me for saying my wicked thoughts but it's true. Kill our ponies? I hated to remember that he had ever said it. Kill our ponies!

I would kill him myself if he ever tried to kill Moonlight! Or Snowball!

Thornburgh camped at the Little Snake River and sent a messenger to White River to tell Meeker he was on his way. The scout was Charlie Lowry, and folks in Rawlins had told Thornburgh that Charlie would be safe, as the Utes all loved his harmonica playing so much.

The Major was asking Meeker for advice and would await Charlie's return message. While waiting, Thornburgh hired Joe Rankin, a livery stable owner in Rawlins, for his guide. No one else in the long wagon train had ever been to White River or had any idea how to get there.

The wagon train, which the Utes had spied, consisted of 153 soldiers and 25 civilians. All those wagons, the Utes believed, were loaded with nooses and handcuffs. This was enough to frighten the young Utes into a frenzy. In reality the wagons were loaded with army rations and supplies for the White River Expedition, not a handcuff in the entire train. But we didn't know that at the time.

I happened to be in Josie's schoolroom next to Meeker's office when Charlie Lowry came clumping in, dusty and weary from the long hard ride. The schoolroom door happened to be open, so I could hear them. All was silent while Meeker read the letter from Thornburgh. Then he shouted.

"Josie! Come here and listen to this!"

As usual, she came at his call. My ear was glued to the crack of the door as he read aloud.

Headquarters, White River Expedition
Camp on Fortification Creek, Sept. 25

Mr. Meeker
U.S. Indian Agent
White River Agency
Sir:

In obedience to instructions from the General of the Army, I am en route to your agency, and expect to arrive there on the 29th instant, for the purpose of rendering you any assistance in my power, and to make arrests at your suggestion, and to hold as prisoners such of your Indians as you desire until investigations are made by your department. I have heard nothing definite from your agency for ten days, and don't know what state of affairs exists; whether the Indians will leave at my approach or show resistance.

I send this letter by Mr. Lowry, one of my guides, and desire you to communicate with me as soon as possible, giving me all the information in your power, in order that I may know what course to pursue. If practicable meet me on the road at the very earliest moment.

Very respectfully, your obedient servant,
T.T. Thornburgh
Major, 4th Infantry, commanding expedition

So! They were on their way! I closed the door softly and ran as fast as I could go to Nicaagat's tipi. He was lying on his lumpy buffalo robe, seeking shade from the heat. In rushing words, I told him of the message as well as I could remember it.

He sat up, as though shot by an arrow.

"Flying Horse," he said. "I want you to saddle up your pony as fast as you can. I may need you to interpret for me. You are going with me to meet Thornburgh."

We were soon on our way to Fortification Creek at a gallop, Nicaagat leading the way. I had never been this way before, as the Yampa Utes always followed the Yampa River to the Shining Mountains on our hunting expeditions. It was all new country for me. In spite of our pressures, I couldn't help drinking in the beauty that surrounded us. The oak bushes had turned to a vivid copper, and the hills were brilliant gold in their aspen colors.

I hadn't been riding on Moonlight for a long time now, and so she was ready to run. I had to hold her back in order to follow the chief. Even though we were riding toward the enemy, just the idea of riding, fast and free through the autumn colors, had a joyful effect on me.

Then we spied them. It looked like hundreds of them, camped under the aspens, with a great many supply wagons scattered through the trees, as far as we could see. Many of the soldiers were standing along the creek banks, fishing. They were obviously at ease. My pulse raced.

"We go back. To Peck's Store. Get all Peck's ammunition for Utes," said Nicaagat. They were the first words spoken since we left the Agency.

We turned back and forded the river, where it was low. We tethered our ponies at the hitching rack in front of the little store. Peck was the Utes' friend who had warned us of Meeker's sending for the troops.

As we entered the darkness of the building, Mrs. Peck greeted us with a warm welcome.

"Chief Jack! Good to see you!"

A man of few words, he got to the point at once.

"Need ammunition. Utes hunting in Wyoming. Buy all." He took paper money from the tobacco pouch hanging at his belt and laid it on the counter. "Where is Peck?"

She lifted a heavy box of cartridges to the counter.

"This is all I have," she said, grunting with the weight of it. "Mr. Peck is due back from Rawlins with a load of supplies for the store any day now. You know the soldiers are going to White River?"

"Utes know." He picked up the big ammunition box, and we walked out into the blinding sun.

"Get on horse," he ordered me. After I was mounted, he hoisted the weight of the box and balanced it on Moonlight's withers. "You carry. We hide it."

We rode slowly back toward the Agency. As we came around the bend in the river, Nicaagat stopped his pony and lifted the huge box from Moonlight's shoulders. Hurriedly he buried it under a pile of aspen leaves that covered the ground.

Then he mounted, whirled, and we rode hurriedly back to the military encampment. This time we rode through the astonished soldiers, our hands up in a sign of peace.

"Where White Chief?" Nicaagat asked the first man we met.

We were escorted immediately to an immense tent, set up in the clearing. Subdued words were exchanged in English, so softly we couldn't hear them. It was obvious the soldiers were very impressed. Most of them were new recruits who had never actually met a "redskin" before. And anyone could see at a glance that this Ute was angry.

A handsome officer got up from a table where he was writing and came quickly toward us. Even I, a Ute, had to admit that he was beautiful, almost as beautiful as Morning Star.

"I am Major Thornburgh," he said. "Commander of the expedition."

"I, Nicaagat, Chief of White River Utes." He cast an eye at me, indicating I was to translate everything. Dutifully I repeated what he said, adding, "Meeker calls him Chief Jack."

"What are you doing here? No need soldiers at White River. All peace there." I continued to repeat it all in English.

Then he went on, pausing occasionally for me to translate.

"Meeker try to make Utes into white man. Plow up pony track. Try to make our children speak English. Go to school. He starve Utes to make us do this. No give Utes supplies we get by treaty."

Thornburgh listened intently to both of us, nodding as though he agreed.

"Meeker tell Utes no can hunt off Reservation. Punishment for setting fires. We no set fires. Fires from drought. Fires from lightning. Utes no set fires. Not fires in forest. No fires in house. No fires in barn."

He then set off on a new track.

"Meeker speak with wicked tongue. Utes no understand him. One day he say something. Next day say different. One day he say he give me new red wagon. Next day he give me old green wagon. Paint falling off."

Thornburgh nodded and shook hands with Nicaagat.

"I admire your honesty," he said. "And I certainly sympathize with you," I translated, "but I have to follow the orders of my superiors."

My heart sank at these words, but I continued to translate.

"General Sherman has ordered me to go to White River to see about all the rumors. I hope you will accompany me to the Agency."

Again he shook hands. And then, as an afterthought, he turned and scooped up a handful of gold-wrapped cigars, handing them to Nicaagat as a parting gift.

Was it to be war? Or peace? Who could tell?

As we turned to leave, Thornburgh called out after us.

"Just a moment!"

Nicaagat turned back.

"You can take this message to Meeker. Tell him we will wait at the boundary of the Reservation for him to arrive and accompany us. We are not making war."

We departed. Could we trust him? We knew we couldn't trust Meeker.

Chapter 13

How could we tell? Would we have war? Or peace, as Nicaagat wanted? I was terrified as we returned to where we had hidden the great box of ammunition under the aspen leaves. We retrieved it and returned to the Agency, exchanging never a word. I don't know if Nicaagat didn't know what to think himself, or whether he considered a woman unsuitable to discuss such matters. I longed to know what he was thinking.

When we finally arrived at the Agency, we found an enormous fat Ute waiting for us – Colorow. He was the only really fat Ute we had ever seen, so we knew before we reached him who it was. Old Biscuit-Eater, as he was known to most of the ranch wives in Colorado, was always begging for biscuits and eating them, uninvited in their kitchens. They owed him that much by treaty, he figured.

Colorow was a Southern Ute whose band had been moved to a Reservation near Denver to save the Government the trouble of sending their rations each month to the Southern Mountains. At first the Utes had been furious and horrified at being jerked up by the roots from their centuries-old homeland and moved to the edge of a white man's city. Then they began to enjoy it. With their treaty money they began to shop for strange things in white man's stores, to laugh in white man's theaters, and go to eat the weird food in white man's restaurants.

But then the government, on another whim, moved Colorow's band again. This time it was to the White River Reservation West of the Shining Mountains. This Reservation was already overcrowded as far as the Utes were concerned. We didn't have enough game as it was, with white men and their busy rifles shooting down more than their share of deer and elk and antelope. Colorow was not happy and neither was his band. Neither were we.

And so we didn't see much of them. The only time they showed up was when rations were doled out. They rode in once a month to get their bags of flour and sugar and coffee that the treaty promised us, and then they disappeared again.

But Old Nick had changed that. He started doling out the meager supplies once a week and on a greatly reduced quantity in order to force the Utes to bend to his will in every way. Colorow and his band were extremely wary of Meeker.

Today Colorow raised his hand in greeting as we rode up.

"Hiya!" he said, but his face didn't show his thoughts. "I hear that Old Nick has sent for the soldiers."

"Soldiers camped at Fortification Creek, waiting to hear form Nick," was Nicaagat's response. "Many, many wagons full of handcuffs and ropes and manacles to carry us away to Indian Territory where Indians go to die. Oklahoma, they call it."

"Not good," agreed Colorow. "Fortification Creek? Four days North."

"Four days left to live." Nicaagat sounded the death bell for the Utes, I thought, my stomach churning. I felt so ill I was afraid I would fall off Moonlight's back. The world seemed to swirl around me in an ugly mixture of blood and darkness. And then my senses seemed to return to me a little.

"I go see Ouray. Utes need him. Fast," Colorow said.

Nicaagat nodded. "Yes. Go!"

Chief Ouray was a great man. If anyone could help us, it must be Ouray. He was the high chief of all Colorado Utes and everyone admired him, Utes and whites alike. He was the chief who had gone to Washington when I was still a little girl. He had signed the treaty with the Great White Father. We thought it was a good treaty at the time, and we all trusted Chief Ouray. But then white men kept tinkering with the treaty until it was now useless.

Another reason we loved Chief Ouray was because Canalla's favorite wife was Susan, Ouray's sister. We felt we were all of the same family.

"Yes. Go! Go!" Nicaagat motioned for Colorow to go. "Fast!"

But Ouray lived on the Uncompahgre Reservation, many days to the South in the high Blue Mountains of Colorado. Colorow would have to fly if he were to get any help from Chief Ouray. Could he do it? Could he get help before we were all dragged off in handcuffs to that horrible Indian Territory where we would be penned up to die?

But whatever happened to Colorow and his wild ride for help, we would die first. We would not allow the soldiers to carry us off. Every tipi on White River Reservation was pledged to die fighting. We would not cause a war. But neither would we allow ourselves to be taken prisoners. We knew the cruelty in white men's hearts. And their determinations to exterminate us like so many rats.

Weren't all the whites in Colorado shouting, "The Utes must go?" It was repeated in every newspaper. It was heard in every speech and statement made by Senator Teller and by Governor Pitkin. We knew that our utter destruction was due by the minute. We were terrified.

Most of us stayed close to our tipis, many of us inside them. But the young warriors were out on their ponies, riding from one tipi to another, their nerves as taut as a bowstring, their anger ready to burst out of control. It was all the elders could do to restrain them.

Thunder Cloud, by nature one of the more restive Utes, was now trying to calm the more violently angry young men.

"Don't shoot!" he rode around the Reservation from one group to another. "That will only bring on our removal sooner. Stay calm!"

I admired my father more that day than I had ever before in my life. It took courage to ride out there among the young warriors, trying to pour cold water on their blazing fury. Especially since most of them carried loaded guns with them.

Little Bear sat crooning softly in our tipi, rocking back and forth as though quieting a baby. She was trying desperately to blot the rumors of destruction carried on the winds of autumn.

And Lone Eagle sat nearby, silently smoking his peach pipe, a cloud of white smoke rising around his head in a telltale story of his anxiety. It was his quiet way of praying for peace. I knew them both so well.

But where was Morning Star? And what was he doing? Was he out there with the other young Utes, ready for battle? I couldn't see him that way, for some reason. I couldn't imagine him wanting to kill anyone, not even a white man. He was too gentle. But what was he doing? We saw him so seldom. He was usually out in the hills, hunting. But today? I prayed he was steering clear of the Fortification Creek area where Thornburgh and his soldiers were camped.

It wasn't until late that afternoon that he rode quietly up to the Agency office and went inside, carrying a letter for Meeker. He was there only briefly before he came out again. I was watching from the flap of my own tipi. I couldn't resist running out to accost him.

"What was the letter?" I whispered.

"I not know," he whispered back. "Letter from Thornburgh, Chief Soldier at Fortification Creek. He say give only to Meeker. But he say not to worry. A good man, I think." He hurried off, leading his pony.

I slipped into Meeker's office, just in time to hear him reading the letter to Josie.

"Don't worry, sir," I caught the words. "I will wait at the border of the Reservation until you come with me to accompany me and my troops, thus avoiding any misunderstanding with the Utes. Thank you for your warning.

"Gratefully yours, T.T. Thornburgh, Major, 4th Infantry, commanding Expedition."

Old Nick heaved a quiet sigh of relief. The old bastard was really afraid for his own life. The holocaust he had created was about to go off in his face, and he wasn't sure how to handle it. Josie sat quietly, offering no help.

"What do you think, daughter?" It wasn't customary for him to ask anyone's advice.

"Do as he asks," was her blunt answer. "Get up to the Reservation boundary as fast as you can!"

"I can't ride a horse! You know that! I never did, and this is no time to start!"

"Well, send a message immediately, then," was her quick response. "By someone you can trust."

"None of my men know the way to Fortification Creek. And I wouldn't trust a Ute! They are a sneaky lot!"

In the habit of seeing me in the office, Josie turned to me.

"Flying Horse, who was that young man who brought Father this letter?"

"Morning Star."

"How did he get this letter?"

"I don't know, ma'am. He is always out hunting. Maybe he met the soldiers up there somewhere."

"Is he a Ute I can trust?" Meeker asked with a sharp edge in his voice.

"Oh, yes, sir! I'm sure he is, sir!"

Then I was embarrassed by my own obvious enthusiasm. Both Josie and her father stared at me with surprise. I felt my cheeks burning.

"Go get him!" was Old Nick's impatient answer.

I fled. Today was no day to "dawdle," I was sure. I soon had Morning Star back in the Agency office.

"Where did you get this letter?" Old Nick acted as though he was going to hang Morning Star. His question was an accusation, blunt and violent. He shook the letter in the young man's face.

The Ute answered in his own tongue, which of course Meeker didn't understand.

"I was hunting antelope. I met the soldiers. They were camped."

"What in the hell is he saying?" Meeker shouted, turning to me. I translated.

"Josie, write a letter for me. My shoulder is in great pain this morning."

She took up a pen and paper at the big desk. He dictated:

Sir:

I have just received your letter of September 27th, delivered by a Ute. You ask me to ride out to meet you on the way. This is impossible, as my presence here is vital to keeping peace with the Indians. They think your coming means war, so I am trying to keep them calm. But keep your troops at the Reservation boundary and come on to the Agency with only five men. That should prove that we haven't declared war.

Respectfully,

N.C. Meeker

She folded and sealed the letter, and Old Nick handed it to Morning Star.

"Deliver this only to Thornburgh!" he shouted at him. He seemed to think that if he shouted loud enough, we could understand the English language. I translated. "And ride fast! This is very urgent!" Again I translated.

Morning Star looked at me as though the message was from me. He smiled slightly and nodded. Then he was gone.

Chapter 14

I was torn and weighted down by this knowledge. I feared for the safety of Morning Star on this hazardous errand. What if something happened to him? I couldn't endure the thought. But even more agonizing was the guilt I felt at concealing this information.

Finally I ran back to our own tipi to find Thunder Cloud. I had to tell him. Tell him for the safety of our people.

"Where is Thunder Cloud?" I asked Little Bear and Lone Eagle, who sat as they had for days, she rocking and crooning, he smoking up a cloud.

"Trying to calm the young warriors," my grandfather answered. "I pray to the Great Father that he succeeds. We can't have war!"

I ran out and sought out Moonlight who was with the rest of the great Ute herd, munching away at even the sage brush, almost starving from the long summer's drought.

Leaping astride her, I rode wildly around the Reservation, hunting for my father. I went to one band of clustered tipis after another. At last I found him, with a group of angry young men around him.

"Tell them, Father!" I shouted. "I have news!"

They all turned to me, surprised. Girls did not interrupt man-talk. Why was I breaking in like this?

"The soldiers are waiting at the edge of the Reservation for word from Old Nick! He has just sent them word that they were not to come inside the Reservation. The chief soldier will come to the Agency with only five men to have a conference. All is safe!"

I added the last words myself, mostly to help Thunder Cloud calm the angry warriors, although I really didn't believe it.

"Thank you, Flying Horse," he thanked me with cool formality, but I could see the love and pride shining in his eyes. I was glad I had come.

It was one more day of peace.

*****

The following morning, just as the Eastern sun was knocking at our tipi doors, I came out in time to see poor, dear Morning Star riding up to the Agency. His pony was obviously exhausted. And so was Morning Star.

I raced to the Agency as fast as my moccasins could carry me, hoping to catch the import of Thornburgh's message. I slipped in behind Morning Star without making a sound. The Meekers were so accustomed to seeing me around that no one paid me any attention.

Old Nick snatched the letter from Morning Star's hand and read aloud to his wife and daughter, who were hovering behind him, both terrified and eager for news.

> Camp on Williams Fork
> September 27, 1879
>
> N.C. Meeker
> Sir:
> I will move my troops to Milk Creek, or some other good place to camp, and will leave them there, as you suggest, and will come to the Agency with only five men.
> Very respectfully, your obedient servant,
> T.T. Thornburgh
> Major, 4th Infantry, Commanding Expedition

Like a flash of lightning, I was out the door and back at my own tipi, where Thunder Cloud was just arising. Breathless, I gave him every word I could remember. He rushed out, rounded up his pony, and was off to spread the news.

"The soldiers would be camped, waiting for word from Meeker!"

One more day of life!

*****

But what we didn't know, and what we didn't find out until it was too late, was that Thornburgh and his other officers had examined the territory and had a troubled conference about what action they should take next.

If they remained at Williams Fork, they would have to enter the Reservation by going through Coal Creek Canyon. They all agreed that this was an ideal place for a Ute ambush, if the Indians were planning to fight. It was a narrow canyon, with inviting cliffs towering overhead, a perfect spot for the Indians to drop tons of rock on top of the troops and even to fire down on them with guns or arrows. It wouldn't be safe to wait, for the Utes might attack at any moment. But how could they get word to Meeker in time for him to know this change in plans? They had no one to carry the message.

It was decided that they must proceed, and quickly. They would cross the boundary into the Reservation but would stop at Milk Creek. From there Thornburgh would go on to the Agency alone, accompanied by only five men. That should not alarm the Utes.

But young warriors were swarming through the hills, alert to any white man's trickery. And they found it, they believed. In no time at all, they thundered up to Chief Nicaagat's tipi with the news.

"Chief!" they were shouting. "White soldiers on Reservation! Now! War! We go fight? Now?"

"No, men! No!" He tried to sooth them. "There is some mistake. You must be mistaken."

"No mistake, Boss! We see them! With our own eyes! They are coming! Hundreds of them! Coming to Agency! Now!"

They were in an insane frenzy, a wild mixture of terror and delight. They knew what they had seen, of course. And what other explanation? The whites, duly warned, had declared open war on the Utes.

All hell seemed to break loose. Chief Nicaagat finally convinced that what the young Utes said was true, rushed to Quinket's tipi for a conference. Both chiefs decided to evacuate all the women, children, and old men immediately to save them from the gruesome extermination that the soldiers had carried out at the Sand Creek Massacre not many years back. It had been too sickening to remember, and yet it was burned into the hearts and minds of every Ute.

Within the hour Quinket had notified every Yampa Ute and Nicaagat every White River Ute to strike camp and head South for Roan Mesa. Before noon every tipi surrounding the Agency, all ninety of them, was gone. The women and old men had pulled down every one of them, packed up their entire belongings on pony drags and were on their way South.

"Don't stop until you get to Old Squaw Camp!" they were warned. "It will be some time before the soldiers can follow you there!"

I was sick with terror before my grandparents and I had torn down our tipi and got it loaded on the travois. How long, I kept thinking. How long did we have to live? But not just for my dear elders was I afraid. And certainly not for myself. My aching heart kept turning back. Back to Thunder Cloud. And to Morning Star. What were they going to do? What would happen to them?

Suddenly I decided. I would stay behind with them. Lone Eagle and Little Bear could go on ahead. I would come later. I knew this was a wild decision. But I had to do it.

"Go!" I urged them. "I will come later! And hurry!"

Suddenly Little Bear was clinging to me and sobbing. This was Little Bear, who was always smiling, or crooning.

"You must come with us! Now!" Her thin little arms squeezed me. Hard! "You cannot stay behind!" she kept whispering.

But I pushed them on their way. I slapped the rump of Little Bear's pony and saw them join the long line of fleeing Indians. All heading South. South for momentary safety. Or perhaps for final extermination. My head roared with the blood throbbing inside it.

But I must find Thunder Cloud. If he were to go out to meet the soldiers, I would go with him. I couldn't let him die alone. Hadn't he allowed me to accompany him on many of his hunting trips up on the Flattops since I was a little girl? Why shouldn't I go with him now on what could be his final hunting trip?

And suddenly, as I roamed around among the confusion of milling horsemen, trying to find him, I remembered Morning Star. Where was he? Was he going out to face the blasting of the soldiers' huge wagon-guns, too? I couldn't imagine it. He was too gentle. But would he be manacled and hauled East to deadly Indian Territory if he didn't fight to the death as the others had sworn to do? My mind thundered with confusing questions. I couldn't sort them out or find answers. I wished I could die, now.

The huge crowd of riders began to thin out, as more and more Utes headed North toward the soldiers who were by now nearing Milk Creek and the Reservation boundary.

"Remember! Don't shoot unless they fire first!" was the shouted warning from the older, wiser men, as the young and fiery ones rushed off to see what was going on at Milk Creek.

It was really more of a sightseeing expedition than anything else. Those who went on ahead were curious. Young and curious, they were eager for anything. They wanted to see real soldiers! They had heard of soldiers all their lives, heard of them with horror and warning. But what were they really like? Copies of Old Nick, more than likely.

But Chief Nicaagat was in the lead of the eager young warriors. He was not going to allow them to make a hasty mistake that could lead to a bloody Ute war. He soon called a halt and let those behind him catch up. He gathered them around him, laying out his strategy in most convincing terms. They would not ride directly toward the creeping military train but would ride off toward a hill near Milk Creek, hide behind it while they watched them crawl past. That way, there would be no confrontation, no battle. And they could count the wagons, count the soldiers, and figure out what they had to contend with.

Nicaagat had charmed them into feeling that they were part of the battle plan. He was a true leader. And so they rode on quietly, making no sound in the early frosty air of Sunday morning. With care they rode behind the ridge that they had chosen as their concealment. But suddenly, contrary to their plan, as they topped the hill, they saw the long line of soldiers coming straight at them. They had changed their minds and had taken a shortcut, thus shattering the Utes' plan.

Although I was not in the lead with the eager warriors, I heard it all in detail from Chief Nicaagat, as he recounted the event long afterward. It was a story we all memorized with sick hearts.

He held out his arm to stop the Utes in their tracks. What now? This he had not expected. Silently they watched the soldiers coming toward them, unaware of the Utes' presence. Determined to maintain peace, Nicaagat kept his hand outstretched, indicating silence. There was no sound in the stillness of the morning except the screeching of the wagon wheels, as the long train rumbled across the rough trail.

Suddenly one of the Ute ponies caught the scent of the horses ahead. He lifted his head high, letting out a shrill whinny that split the air like a war whoop.

The soldiers looked up, seeing the group of Utes lined up along the brow of the hill. Some of them wore battered cowboy hats, some with a lone eagle feather tucked in their headbands. The soldiers were probably as startled as the Utes. All movement ceased. Each group watched the other with wary anxiety.

Nicaagat, with sensitive ears turned to the light wind from the valley, caught the words of a distant voice.

"It's Chief Jack's band, Major!" said Joe Lawson, the guide for the expedition. "Start shootin'! They've set up an ambush!"

Instead, Thornburgh rode out alone from his men, waving his hat to indicate peace. At the same time, two Utes on foot started walking down the hill to the white men. It was Nicaagat and a cool young Uncompahgre Ute, who had come to the White River Agency to court a certain young woman he'd fallen in love with. Both held out their hands in peace.

Suddenly, without warning, a shot rang out. Which side it came from, no one ever knew. But the Battle of Milk Creek had begun.

Thornburgh, shot through the head, slipped from his horse. He was dead before he ever touched the Earth.

C h a p t e r   1 5

I could hear the ugly rattle of guns long before I reached Milk Creek. The war had begun! My heart felt as though a knife had cut through it. This was the end! I kicked Moonlight with cruel urgency in the ribs. Hurry! I had to hurry! I had to find Thunder Cloud. I had to keep him safe somehow.

As I topped the ridge I could see the battle going on below. The soldiers were pulling their wagons around in a huge circle at the edge of the golden aspen grove behind them. Many of them were already inside the circle, digging what seemed to be a great pit. But there were many more outside, their rifles trained on the hillside below me.

Suddenly I found it! Thunder Cloud's pinto pony! And Father was on his back, charging into the thick of the battle. Oh, Thunder Cloud, please! Please come back! I prayed.

I knew he wouldn't, even as I was praying. Not Thunder Cloud. Now that the war started, he would not turn back. He had pledged to fight to the death, rather than submit to white man's manacles. I hadn't pledged. What could I do? But I had to stop him.

With blind abandon I drove Moonlight charging down the hillside toward Thunder Cloud. Spurts of dust were popping up around us. I dare not stop now. And then I was beside him.

"Thunder Cloud!" I shouted. "Come back!"

He whirled at the sound of my voice. Was it anger or was it terror that twisted his face when he saw me? It was not a pleasant sight.

"Go back!" he bellowed. "Go back to the Agency this minute! Do you understand me?"

Never had he spoken to me like this in my life. I was stunned. What had I done? Fury had turned his face white under the sunburn of his dark skin.

"Do you understand?" he repeated. "Go back to the Agency! And stay there!"

Those were the last words he ever spoke. At that moment a bullet hit him from behind. He toppled headlong from his pony. I had to leave him lying there among the bullets and the puffs of dust. I had to go back to the Agency. Now! As he had said.

I turned and fled back up the hill through the hail of bullets. I wondered if one of them might strike Moonlight. God, no! Or maybe even me? I would have welcomed that. Spirit in the Sky, take me too!

And then we were over the hill and behind it. The shooting seemed very far away. But still I kicked Moonlight in the ribs, urging her on.

I expected the Agency to be totally abandoned. Empty. Deserted. I was surprised to see several young Utes rushing about, guns in hand. One of them stopped short just in front of me. His long rifle was pointed at the barn. My eyes followed his aim. There, coming out of the barn, was Shadrach Price. A blast from the Ute's gun and Shad Price fell dead without even a twitch. Then I could see what was going on at every Agency building. Every white man was doomed.

Another shot and I saw William Post, Meeker's friend from Yonkers, New York, fall in the doorway of the storeroom, a sack of flour still in his arms. Other shots blasted the stillness. I was nauseated, ready to vomit.

What was happening to the women? I hadn't long to wait, for Persune came from Meeker's office with poor Josie in his arms. He carried her gently to his pony that was tied to the hitching rack. In rank contrast to the way the other whites were being slaughtered, he placed Josie tenderly upon his pony's back.

"Now!" he exulted. "You mine! Persune's wife!"

She kept her head bowed, shame and fear struggling in her pale face. She was no doubt thinking of his other two wives. She looked as sick as I felt.

I was shocked to see Canalla coming out the kitchen door, still in his battered plug hat. He was shoving Flora Ellen Price ahead of him, with her tiny blond children still clinging to her skirts, sobbing. Not Canalla, our noble Medicine Man! I couldn't believe the truth of my own eyes. Here was not some hot-blooded young Ute on the warpath. Here was Chief "Johnson," as the whites called him. I held my hands tight over my retching mouth. Not Canalla!

I realized that this was war – real and hideous war. And the hatred in war engulfed everyone. We were all drowning in it. No one was exempt.

And finally came Quinket, Chief "Douglas," our gentle Yampa Ute. By one arm he was dragging Arvilla Meeker, like a limp rag doll. He was walking so fast, she had no time to get to her own feet. It looked as though he were going to discard her on the garbage heap at the kitchen door. But my other senses told me that he had other uses for her. She would have preferred the garbage heap, I'm sure.

Suddenly a bloodcurdling shriek split the early Sunday silence. It was Arvilla. She jerked free of her captor's grasp and stumbled to her feet. She had spied the naked body of her dead husband at the corner of the Agency. She rushed to him, bending over him in tender devotion. Even I, who had long held her in bitter contempt, felt a pang of sympathy for her.

She bent to kiss him, but what she saw stopped her in horror. A stave from a flour barrel had been jabbed down his throat. And a heavy log-chain was fastened around his naked neck. It was evident that the Utes would later drag his body around the premises, as he had so often threatened that the Utes would be dragged to Indian Territory.

She fainted dead away. Quinket picked her up roughly and threw her across the back of a nearby pony. Her head dangled toward the Earth. Poor old Arvilla. Even I could no longer be angry with her. Nor with Old Nick. I turned away and vomited.

*****

The next days were a nightmare. To tell you the truth, I cannot even remember them or what exactly happened. Strangely enough, I can recall the morning of the massacre before I rode off to follow Thunder Cloud to the battle at Milk Creek, but I can't drag up any clear memories of the days that followed.

I can remember before the fighting started that Old Nick was fighting with Canalla about refusing to issue the regular annuity blankets for the Utes' fall hunting trip up into Wyoming. And I remember Meeker fighting with Chief Quinket over his request for guest rations for Yanko, the Ute from Chief Ouray's band who was up to court a girl in our band. Old Nick was in a foul mood with everyone at the Agency. That I can remember.

And I have vague troubled memories of our setting off after the fleeing elders, women and children, as they hurried South toward Piceance Creek and Roan Mesa. I remember they had been warned not to stop until they reached Old Squaw Camp.

I remember only that there was a great bright moon that night, and I could see Quinket keep tipping up a bottle of liquor to his mouth, taking a deep drink and then holding it up to the moon to measure what was left. He had to drink, I guess, to give him the courage to do what he was doing. It was all so against his principles. I realize now that he was quite drunk that night, with poor Arvilla riding painfully behind him on the pony.

I don't quite remember when I discovered that she had been shot in the hip during the massacre and that the wound was still bleeding. When I saw Josie trying to dress the wound the following week, I helped with it, more for Josie's anxiety than for her mother's pain, I'm afraid. I knew of some Ute herbs that we used for wounds.

By that time, our fleeing band had topped the divide as we crossed over the western slope to the Grand River below us. We could slow down in our wild escape from the soldiers now and pitch camp until our own warriors could rejoin us. We had left Old Squaw Camp far behind us.

I hadn't realized that Yanko, the Uncompahgre Ute who had been at White River courting his ladylove when the massacre took place, had left us. But I was alert to his return, riding pell-mell into camp late one night, his pony in foaming lather. He carried a message from Chief Ouray from his ranch in the mountains to the South.

"Stop shooting the whites immediately!" was the message. "All trouble must stop!" Josie read it aloud to me, and I translated to the Utes crowding around us. Oh, how I longed to have Thunder Cloud with us to help us decide what to do. He was so wise.

Ouray was practically idolized by all the Utes of Colorado, but this powerful message raised a groan from the assembled group. War was war. How could we stop now? The soldiers had broken their word not to cross the Reservation boundary, hadn't they? They had invaded us. We were entitled to fight to protect our own lives. Right was right.

The anger at our great leader boiled up in the arid heat of the night. It was the young warriors, returning from the actual battlefield at Milk Creek, whose anger flared. But it was the calm leadership of our own chief, Nicaagat, which quieted them.

"Hear me, brothers," he said. "Our warriors are returning. Our war is over, as far as we are concerned. We are ready for peace."

Still the growling continued. Undercurrents of smothered anger. How dare Chief Ouray demand that we lay down our arms?

"Enough, my good men," Nicaagat went on quietly. "We have upheld the Ute honor as our rules demand. We have won our war."

"But what of the women?" an angry young voice shouted from the edge of the crowd. "Are we going to treat them like gods?"

Other voices and echoes repeated the agitation that this question aroused. "Hi-yah! The women! The women!"

My heart shriveled. I found it hard to breathe.

Nicaagat was silent. He raised his deep-set eyes to the West, where the last faint rays of daylight outlined the rising of Grand Mesa across the river valley. He had no words. There was only a painful silence.

Then our Yampa Chief, Quinket, came forward and stood beside Nicaagat. He looked very small and very old, as he stood there, his graying mustache looking white in this dim light. But he spoke out with courage.

"I know what you are thinking. You have questioned how we have treated the white women that we are holding captives. Right?"

"Hi! Hi! Hi!" raised the chorus.

"We promise you, my brothers. They have been properly humiliated, as is our law. Each has been violated. So go now, in peace. We have won the war."

Chapter 16

But we had not won the war, we soon discovered. We had no more than got our village set up at what we considered a safe distance from the White River Agency, than a Ute runner staggered in to camp one morning early. He could scarcely speak from the weight of his terrifying message.

The soldiers were on the march again, this time determined to destroy the Utes completely. Colonel Wesley Merritt, Commander of the Fifth United States Cavalry at Fort Russell, had replaced Thornburgh. The soldiers were on our trail, and they would not stop until they had exterminated us or chased us from the state of Colorado.

Again we were horrified, ready to explode. Even the fiery young warriors knew that we were heavily out-gunned. Any fighting would indeed have to be a fight to the death, for with the new reinforcements from Fort Russell, we would be deficient in ammunition as well as warriors. In spite of their pledges to fight to the death, the young warriors weren't quite ready to die... yet! The desire to live a bit longer was too strong.

So again we pulled down our newly set-up village on Roan Mesa and set off as fast as we could travel, down the westward slope toward the Grand River. But now it was our captives who seemed to slow us down. Persune refused to travel fast as the train of heavily loaded ponies pushed down to Rifle Creek. He didn't say so, but we knew he was trying to protect Josie from the hard ride. She was his woman now. His wife. It turned me sick.

Quinket was not in the least concerned about the comfort of his elderly and wounded prisoner. His urgency was apparent, as he rode along the pack train pushing each family to the limit.

"Hurry! Hurry!" he repeated, over and over again. Even Canalla, burdened by his captives, was not as eager to escape as the old Chief.

Flora Ellen's small children, also frightened and weary, held us back with their crying and hysterics. But our Medicine Man was patient and often took their childish needs into consideration.

Quinket was frantic still. We could now see the great Bookcliffs looming high to our right, like giant copies of Arvilla's *Pilgrim's Progress* stacked up into mountains. They spurred us on.

And then it was Quinket himself who was lagging behind, for his intense anxiety had apparently affected his own little girl, Mariposa. She developed a raging fever. When she wasn't lying in a coma, she was screaming in terror, in mad dreams of the "whites."

"Don't let them get me!" she would suddenly shriek, day and night. Quinket was nearly as distraught as she, just hearing the terror in her voice. Mariposa was his pet, his favorite, just as I had been for Thunder Cloud. Her hysteria hurt me as much as it did our old Chief, I think, for it brought my beloved father back again to that ghastly hillside at Milk Creek where I had left him lying. Was his poor body still there? Hot tears wet my cheeks.

The second night off Roan Plateau, we were camped in a hurried makeshift camp along upper Piceance Creek. Mariposa's crying was keeping us all on edge. I sat up just in time to see Arvilla Meeker limping from her own blanket over to Mariposa's mother, who was rocking and crooning to the child. She carried a mug from her meager pack and held it to the child's lips.

"Here. Drink, my dear," I heard her whisper, stroking the hot forehead of the little girl. "This will help you sleep."

Quinket sat on his own blanket, watching, ready to snatch the cup from her hand. For a moment, I thought he would, for his hand jerked involuntarily toward the mug. Then he restrained himself.

Mariposa drank thirstily and then sank back into her mother's arms. That was the last of her delirium. Whatever the medicine that Arvilla had given her, it worked. We were able to start out again the next morning according to plan. Still pale and frightened, she rode on her mother's pony-drag with wide-open understanding eyes. But her illness was gone.

I couldn't help but notice that this morning, Quinket put his own saddle on Arvilla's pony and even added his own cat-skin sleeping pillow to the saddle to ease her aching hip.

Two days later we reached the Grand River. In the hubbub and confusion of getting us across, young Utes, elderly Utes, pony-drags laden with tipis and luggage and the very few extra ponies we were able to bring along...in all this madness, I was able to approach dear Josie for the first time since the massacre.

"How are you, dear friend?" I whispered, bringing her free hand to my lips.

"Oh, Mollie, darling!" Her face lighted up like the sun coming up in the morning. She threw her arms around me, but then suddenly recovered herself, remembering that she and I were now supposed to be enemies.

Without another word, she quickly put her hand into her skirt pocket and then slipped something into my hand. She gave me an urgent push, as though to shove me away. I took the hint and walked off, joining the others wading their skittish ponies into the roaring current of the Grand River.

Moonlight plunged into the water, sending up a great splashing as she lunged wildly across. "Thank the Great Spirit it is not spring high water, as it used to be on the upper Yampa!" I prayed silently.

Then I stole a quick moment to read the note I held in my hand. I was so glad that I had learned to decipher Josie's neat handwriting in those long months I had studied in her classroom.

"Dear Friends at Uintah Ute Agency," she had written. "Please send help to rescue three women captives, taken hostage at the White River Agency massacre on September 29, 1879. I fear we shall not survive if we do not get help soon. We also have two small children with us. Time is urgent. Signed, Josephine Meeker, daughter of Nathan Meeker, White River Agent."

Consternation cut off my breathing. Holy Father in the Sky! Josie was sending me to save her! Help me! Help me! How would I go about it? What would I do now? I was stricken with terror. What should I do first? There was no one to ask. I thrust the note hurriedly into the pouch at my belt.

I knew that the Uintah Ute Agency was off in the West somewhere, far, far off. No one I knew had ever been there, but the Utes had spread the word that life for the Uintah's was even more difficult than it was for the White River Utes with Meeker.

The Great White Father in Uintah Land was a man with a good heart, they said, a man by the name of Brigham Young, who had brought his people, wagon after wagonload of them, hundreds of days from the East. He had befriended the Indians who lived in the Valley of the Great Salt Lake. They liked him.

"It is cheaper to feed the Utes than it is to fight them," he told his followers. But many of the Mormons, as they were called, did not agree. And so we knew, through Ute hearsay, that there were good Mormons, like their Great Father. But we were also frightened by the stories of the terrible atrocities of the Black Hawk War, as the white men called it.

I had grown up on the terrifying stories of poor Black Hawk, the Ute Chief who had fought desperately to save his people from starvation. These things were happening while I was still a little girl, so the stories around the fires at night were still fresh from the battlefields. We worshiped Black Hawk, the great Ute Chief. He was our hero, for he was fighting against the same terrors the white man was beginning to inflict on us. The Uintah Utes too had been driven into poverty, their game killed by white guns, their land destroyed by the hoofs of ten thousands of cattle, their religion and culture humiliated, and their lives smashed.

Black Hawk tried to arrange a counsel with the Mormons at Manti, hoping to work out some kind of a solution. But the whites refused the invitation. So the Utes planned their own vengeance. They stole thousands of head of cattle and horses, which they sold in New Mexico and Colorado Territory, making their own kind of victory.

I still remembered shivering as I listened to the bloody stories from the Black Hawk War. I remembered one in particular, and I shivered again. Clutching Josie's note, I recalled the oft-told story of the Ute captives being held at Circleville in the town's meetinghouse. As a terrified child, I had shuddered at the brutal fate of the poor Indians, as the Mormons slit the throats of three Ute men, five Ute women, and two Ute children. The Black Hawk War lasted seven years, piling up many horror stories, until it ended with a bullet in Black Hawk's stomach.

And yet my beloved Josie was now asking me to ride into this unknown land of the Uintah Utes. How would I know the way? Who could I turn to? Alone. I would have to do it alone. When? Now!

I glanced at the sun, measuring how much of the day was already gone. It was mid-morning. And in this wild confusion of crossing the Grand River, my escape might not be noticed. The purple mass of Grand Mesa loomed to the South of us, the Utes' destination. Surely Merritt's pursuing army could not find us there, in its labyrinth of tangled cliffs and canyons.

But which way was I to ride? My vague knowledge of the area made me feel as though I were heading into a blinding snowstorm. Something in the back of my mind told me "West." West along the Grand River. West, West, West to the Land of the Uintahs. Would I ever find the Agency? I had to try. The lives of Josie and Arvilla and Flora Ellen and her children depended on me!

Encouraging Moonlight with a gentle pat on the neck, we headed West, along the south bank of the Grand. I looked straight ahead, hoping anyone seeing me would think I was searching a hidden place to relieve myself. We would keep riding until we were safely out of sight. I loosened the reins on Moonlight's neck and she hurried her pace, delighted to be freed again. She raised her head and snorted with pleasure. Perhaps a race lay ahead?

Yes. A race lay ahead. A race for life.

Chapter 17

It was late afternoon by the time my belly began to growl with hunger. I had ridden through miles of rough territory along the bank of the Grand River before I seriously began looking for a bit of food. How far would I have to go?

Far ahead I spied a heavy patch of chokecherry bushes along the riverbank. It was now October, and the green leaves had long ago fallen in shades of orange and yellow. But maybe there might be a few cherries left on the twigs.

I rode on. Moonlight's excitement for a possible race had long since subsided. She lagged, although I kept urging her on with my heels. She was tiring. I was, too, but I kept her at a gallop until she was in a foaming lather. I had to hurry, before my people, in their terror and revenge, slit the throats of Josie and the others!

Dare I stop even for a stray chokecherry?

Suddenly a shadow of movement across the river caught my eye. I pulled Moonlight up short, and while she stood panting, I stared at the area where I had seen something. Something moving. What was it? Fright choked in my throat.

I continued to stare. What had it been? I could see nothing but a barren riverbank, sometimes a cluster of bare bushes, or a sharp cliff, sloughing off into the swift current. Nothing. I continued to scour the opposite bank, scarcely breathing. Was I imagining things? Perhaps I was too tired. Were there evil spirits haunting me? Perhaps the wicked Little People, of whom we had often heard, were nearby.

I stroked poor Moonlight's sweating neck. Poor, dear Moonlight. I was putting her through white man's Hell, I knew.

Her head was sagging. Maybe I should take it easy for a while. And then I patted the pouch at my belt. How could I? There was so little time.

All at once Moonlight's head jerked erect, and her ears shot forward. Her head whirled to stare across the river. She uttered an ear-splitting neigh. She was greeting another horse!

I was right! There was indeed someone across the river. But who? I was afraid I was going to topple from Moonlight's back in sheer terror. Who was there? I still could see no one.

After what seemed an eternity, I suddenly came to my senses. What should I do? I had to push on. And fast! I had to save Josie!

I jerked Moonlight's head around and headed West. We must push West. We had to get to the Uintah Agency, wherever that was. The sun was getting low in the sky. The purple immensity of Grand Mesa towered to my left. That was where the Utes were carrying the prisoners. Could I save them in time?

I dug my heels into Moonlight's ribs. But instead of guiding her, I let her find her own way. My attention was still across the river. For a brief moment, I caught a glimpse of a horseman. And then he was gone.

The sun sank behind the rim of the Earth. Night began to fall. I stared across the river, but the light was failing. I could see very little as the twilight filled in the river valley with darkness. Grand Mesa still loomed like an oppressive menace over my shoulder. I kept thinking of it as the final resting place of dear, Josie, with her throat cut. I urged Moonlight on.

I ached from head to heels. I longed for my lumpy buffalo pad, packed on the pony-drag with Lone Eagle and Little Bear. But the thought didn't last long. Instead my mind was on the strange horseman across the river, upon the Uintah Agency, and upon Josie. Dear, laughing Josie. Always Josie. Would I be in time?

Night closed in on me. Deep black night. We no longer traveled fast. In fact, we scarcely crawled. I even let Moonlight stop and breathe for a bit occasionally. Poor Moonlight. She stumbled often. I pulled her up to give her another rest.

And suddenly it was morning. Dawn was painting the East a soft tender pink. How long I had slept on Moonlight's back, I had no idea. But tomorrow was here. And I was clinging to the white hair of the horse's mane. And her head was sagging near her feet.

I pulled her head up, and we started on. I stared across the river, searching for the ominous stranger. There was nothing. I felt as though I had dreamed it. Perhaps I had.

I slowly noticed that the river had made a bend toward the North during my night ride. I was losing time by following it, if I were to reach the Uintah Agency in time. I had to cross it again. Now. No telling how much time and distance I had already lost.

I began searching for a place where I could safely ford. It was the time of year when the water was low, but even then it was enough to frighten Moonlight. She had never recovered from the fright she had when we lost Snowball in the raging Yampa. I hated to force her into the Grand while she was so nearly exhausted from yesterday's wild ride. Poor, dear pony!

I finally found a spot where the Grand was wide and calm. It seemed a very long way across, but I thought this would be better than plunging into deep, swift water. I urged her in, greatly against her will. But we moved slowly and steadily across. She shied only once, frightened by a floating branch that seemed to attack her from the right.

And then we were across. She lunged hurriedly up the bank, as though a wild wolf were snapping at her heels. I let her stop to rest a moment as I patted her neck and sang Little Bear's crooning song to her. I got my bearings from the sun and headed straight

West. I had no idea how to find the Agency, but I knew it was in Mormon country. If I kept riding long enough, I might find it. I had to try. Poor, dear Josie!

I prayed I wouldn't find any Mormons. Not the kind with sharp knives and cruel hearts! My hand went to my throat involuntarily. As I thought of them, terror made me dizzy. Or maybe it was hunger. I clung to Moonlight's mane and rode on.

The sun climbed the sky. Moonlight picked up her pace a little, as though escaping that terrible river behind her. She had been glad enough to pause and drink from it yesterday, but now she just wanted to escape.

Suddenly I heard the clatter of hoofs behind me. An icy hand seemed to grip my heart. I couldn't breathe. I couldn't turn my head. It was that horrible stranger from yesterday.

I forced myself to turn. It was a rider, coming at a frantic pace. It was Morning Star! Morning Star...on his buckskin pony! I burst into ridiculous tears. Dear Morning Star! Why should I cry now? Crazy, I must have been!

I pulled Moonlight up short and waited. Tears rolled down my cheeks. I tried to wipe them away before he could see them. He would scorn this childish display. What would he think of me?

And then he was beside me, and I was in his arms, even as we sat our ponies.

"Oh, Morning Star!" I sobbed. "Thank our Great Sky Father it is you. I was so afraid. So afraid last night. I was afraid it might have been one of the Mormons!"

"Don't cry, Little One," he whispered as he stroked my wild flying hair. "Don't cry."

Finally I pulled myself up straight and stared at him. "Why are you here?" I asked.

"I followed you."

"But why?"

"I saw you ride away at the crossing yesterday."

"But why did you follow me?"

"I didn't know where you were going. And I wondered if you knew where you were going. You don't know how dangerous it is out here away from the tribe!"

"Oh, dear Morning Star," I whispered, pressing my cheek against his. "Thank you for coming! I am riding with a note to the Uintah Agent from Josie Meeker. And I don't know the way!"

I am ashamed to admit it, but I started crying again. I can't tell you why. It was such a relief to have him there.

His face seemed to darken. "A note? From Meeker?" he asked.

"From Josie. She's asking the Agent at Uintah to save them. Before the Utes kill them."

Again he stroked my hair without speaking. A long time he had no words. Finally he spoke.

"You go back now. I will take the note."

I pulled myself up straight again. I looked at him, sitting so tall and handsome upon his buckskin pony. He was doing this for me. He scarcely even knew Josie.

"Do you know the way?"

"No, but neither do you. It is not safe out here alone for a woman."

"And not for a man, either. Remember the Mormons and the Black Hawk War."

He looked at me anxiously.

"Can you trail the tribe up on to Grand Mesa? Alone?" he asked.

"Of course!" I didn't mean to but I'm afraid I sounded a bit angry.

"Go now," he whispered into my hair. "And may the Great Father go with you." He took the pouch and note from my hand.

I watched him ride off toward Mormon Land. And again, I couldn't hold back my tears.

"Hurry! Please hurry!" I said aloud. I knew that Colonel Merritt's army was getting closer to the fleeing Utes and their captives. Could Morning Star find the Uintah Agency and get help in time?

Chapter 18

What I didn't know, as I slowly retraced my trail up the Grand River, was that help was coming from another direction. We knew Merritt's army was pursuing us from Roan Plateau, and that they were hot on our heels. As they neared the fleeing Utes, I knew that Josie's chances of living were shrinking by the minute.

It had been almost three weeks now since the ghastly massacre. How much longer could the terrorized young warriors be restrained by our older and wiser chiefs, Quinket and Nicaagat, and by our Medicine Man, Canalla? These three were the ones who held the lives of Josie and Arvilla and Flora Ellen and her children in their hands. How much longer could they hold out?

But from the South, another group was approaching. Chief Ouray, the greatest chief of all Colorado Utes, was assembling a rescue mission at his ranch home near Los Piños Agency on the Uncompahgre River. Leading them was General Adams, the government agent who had once been an Indian Agent and was very fond of the Utes.

Chief Ouray was sending along his most trusted messenger, Yanko, as well as his brother-in-law, Sapovanero, and his war chief, Shavano. In all there were five whites and thirteen Uncompahgre Utes. Ouray himself was too ill to go, as his life was coming to an early end as a result of severe kidney disease. He was now so thin and weak he could scarcely sit up. But he was determined to save the captives.

At his elbow, helping him plan the rescue was his wife, Chipeta. In earlier years, while Chief Ouray was traveling to Washington and signing national Ute treaties, lovely Chipeta had charmed America with her dimpled beauty, graciousness, and wisdom. But now she was a very weary, very worried, middle-aged woman. Her heart lay with the Ute captives on Grand Mesa.

She arranged to send along her own buckboard in which to carry back the white women. But it had to be left behind when the rescue party decided to take a murderous short cut across Grand Mesa. Old Shavano knew a deer trail that saved them twenty miles and made it more than worthwhile.

Poor Yanko had his trouble, too, we learned later. The mule team pulling the supply wagon balked at crossing a ravine. The two white men from Los Piños Agency became hysterical with trying to get the mules to move. They beat them unmercifully. Finally one man broke into tears. Still the mules balked. Finally Yanko got the mules moving using his own pony as leader.

"White man... big pain!" was his disgusted remark.

* * * * *

With bone-aching weariness I retraced my way up-river to the crossing of the Grand. And I think Moonlight was as exhausted as I was. At one moment my heart said, "Poor pony! Don't push her. She needs a rest!" But a moment later I heard another voice calling. It was Josie's, calling, "Hurry! Hurry! Merritt's army is overtaking us! Help! Please help...while we are still living!"

The Ute trail was not hard to follow, as the hoofs of dripping ponies left their prints out of the river. And it was no trouble to find the trail of the many travois, cutting into the Earth as the Utes climbed up toward the massive top of Grand Mesa. Stubbornly I pushed on although my eyes were getting bleary with weariness. At times I could hardly see. But I knew that Merritt and his soldiers were at my heels. I had to press on. I knew that his orders were to exterminate the Utes.

And then it was night again. I seemed to have lost track of time, even of day and night. I was sick from hunger and weariness. I saw strange shadows moving around me, shadows that weren't there I discovered when I shook my head hard and cleared my eyes. Moonlight drank deeply from a little stream in the darkness. I slipped from her back and slumped against a nearby tree trunk. I slept.

With the sun suddenly warming my face, I awoke. Below me spread a widening valley. My eyes cleared. And there, in the distance, were clusters of tipis. And ponies grazing. And slender threads of campfire smoke climbing into the autumn sky. And small brown children racing about the dry meadow, chasing one another. And Ute women with packs of dry wood on their backs. There were no warriors to be seen. No men at all. It was a peaceful and heartwarming sight.

With aching joints, I climbed up on Moonlight's back and headed down into the valley as fast as I could go. They were safe! At least for the time being. If something had happened to Josie, the scene wouldn't look this way, I was sure.

As I neared the encampment, I recognized my own tipi, with Little Bear stirring a pot of beans over the fire. As I rode up, her mouth dropped open in astonishment.

"Flying Horse, where in the world have you been? We feared you had been captured by the soldiers!"

I managed to laugh a little to ease her worries. "No, blessed Mother. I was carrying a little message for Josie. Nothing to fear."

But I didn't pause. I was anxious to tell Josie that her note was on the way. I had to ride to the far edge of camp before I located Persune's tipi. I recognized it by his two squaws, who stood holding a blanket before the opening.

"Josie?" I called softly.

The blanket was pushed aside and she came rushing out, joy and questions lighting up her face. I slipped off Moonlight's back and into her outstretched arms.

"Did you...?" she broke off, not knowing how to word the question burning in her heart.

"Yes," I whispered. "Morning Star has your message with him. He is now in Mormon Land."

"I pray he gets help in time," she whispered, but some of the anxiety faded from her face.

And then we heard the uneasy voices of some Ute children, running back to their mothers with a warning.

"The whites are coming!" they shrieked. "The whites are coming!"

Josie and I clutched each other in terror. Merritt's soldiers had overtaken us! The children ran screaming into their mothers' arms. I spied the outline of riders moving across the top of the hill and into the valley.

"Oh, my God!" Josie prayed. "Save us! Save us, dear God!"

Everyone in the encampment seemed to be frozen in time. No one moved, except the terrified children as they disappeared into the tipis. Our eyes were glued to the approaching horsemen.

All at once the trapped breath escaped my lips. A sigh of relief brought me back to breathing again. It was not the soldiers. It was a mixed group of whites and Utes. I recognized Yanko, the Uncompahgre Ute who had visited the White River Agency so often. This was a rescue party from Chief Ouray.

The whole camp seemed to explode with welcome and excitement. We all rushed to greet the newcomers. Our relief was without bounds. Best of all was the presence of General Adams, whom we all remembered as the government man who was a friend of the Utes for many years.

Yanko spied Josie and rode hurriedly toward us.

"You all right, Miss?" He spoke a little English. But before she could answer, General Adams rode up, his kindly face a welcome sight.

"Oh, you poor dear child!" he exclaimed. "Are you all right?"

"As well as can be expected, under the circumstances."

"Do you know who killed your father?"

Of course, everyone in America knew the grisly story by now. It had been twenty-three days since the massacre, and Governor Pitkin lost no time in publicizing his favorite motto, "The Utes must go!"

"No, sir. We didn't see it happen."

"Please forgive me, but I must ask a very personal question before the others come. Did the Utes treat you well?"

"About as well as we expected."

"I mean...you know...did they respect your person?" He was very ill at ease.

"Oh, yes, of course," was her hurried response. But it didn't seem to ring true.

"How is your mother? Where is she?"

"She's in Chief Douglas' tipi, wherever that is. She's been quite miserable."

"And the Price woman? And her children? How did they survive?"

"Oh, they're fine! Chief Johnson keeps them in his tipi."

"Johnson? Oh, you mean Canalla, the Medicine Man?"

"Yes. Papa couldn't remember the Ute names, so he named them himself."

"And where is Canalla's tipi?"

"I'm not sure, sir. We haven't been camped long enough to know. But I think it is farther down in the woods."

As he turned to ride off into the woods, a happy sight greeted him. Susan, Ouray's sister, was walking toward them, smiling broadly, with little Johnnie Price strapped to her back. He was happily sucking on a piece of dried venison. Ahead of her ran little May Price, her blond hair freshly brushed and shining golden in the sun. Flora Ellen walked behind, looking calm and contented.

Susan had apparently accepted the Prices as part of hers and Canalla's family, just as any good Ute wife should. The world seemed happy.

But it only looked that way. This peace was only temporary.

C h a p t e r   1 9

Quinket soon arrived at his tipi to discover General Adams sitting beside Arvilla, who lay in her buffalo-pad bed, her face pale and gaunt. She was tortured by her wounded hip and by the unkindness of Quinket's wives.

Quinket arrived in a fury. What right did these arrogant white men have in the privacy of his tipi? The fact that the white was an old friend, General Adams, didn't do anything to calm his anger. Didn't the fool know that his young braves were bursting to attack the whites?

Adams arose, holding out his hand in friendly greeting. The chief ignored the proffered hand.

"Whites not welcome in my lodge," was his rude reply. This was not like him, who had always been a friendly ally of the whites. But war makes strangers of old friends.

"I came to you to have a council about your prisoners. Can we talk?"

"No. Not until my men come from other camp. Maybe we talk then. Maybe."

Soon a group of White River Utes rode over the hill and down into the valley, armed with rifles and bows. They were prepared for trouble. Their faces were heavy with angry scowls. All of us froze where we sat, waiting. When would the shooting begin? The pounding of my heart could be heard outside my body, I knew. Would it be another Milk Creek battle? I thought of Thunder Cloud.

There was a long conference among the Utes. We waited, watching. Then the Indians sat in front of Quinket's tipi in a huddled group, staring at the whites. Quinket indicated his curt invitation for the whites to join them.

The wrangling began with the sun high overhead. We were too far away to hear anything that was said. We could only watch. And pray. All afternoon the arguing went on. Quinket and his Utes remained stubbornly angry. General Adams remained stubbornly calm.

At last I could hold my anxiety no longer. I began to move closer to the council as the sun fell behind the purple shadows of Grand Mesa. I was in the shadow, where I hoped I would not be seen. But I had to hear them! I had to!

Finally I could catch their words in the silence of the valley. Quinket repeated over and over that the Utes would release the captives as soon as Adams went to White River and stopped Merritt's soldiers from their advance South. Adams kept refusing to go to White River until the captives were released and sent to Ouray.

The sun slid behind the mountains and an orange glow painted the western sky. Still the haggling continued. I could tell by the sag in General Adams' shoulders that he was discouraged. He felt he had failed, I knew.

"Don't give up!" I prayed. "Don't give up!"

Finally Sapovanero, Chief Ouray's brother-in-law, got slowly to his feet. Everyone turned to stare at him.

"We have heard enough," was his quiet announcement. "I am here to speak for Chief Ouray, head of all the Utes. He sent me with this message. Today is Tuesday. If the captives are not freed and at his farm by Friday, he will bring the full force of all Uncompahgre Utes to take the captives by force. And then he will go on to drive you into the guns of Merritt's army. That is my message from Ouray." He sat down and folded his arms.

There was an agonizing silence. No one dared speak. At last Quinket spoke up, uncertainly. His question was directed straight at Adams.

"You sure you can stop soldiers?"

"I am on this mission by the authority of President Hayes. I think Colonel Merritt will listen to me."

Slowly his weary eyes circled the group of Utes, waiting for each to give his sign of agreement. Every Ute finally gave his assent. Adams uttered a soft sigh of relief.

"Thank you, my friends," he said, as he pulled his watch from his pocket. "Five o'clock. Sapovanero and I will go on to White River as soon as we have a bite of supper. There will be a bright moon tonight so we can see the trail. First thing tomorrow morning, Captain Cline

from Los Piños Agency will take the prisoners back to where you left the wagons. From there, he and the Uncompahgre Utes will take them back to Ouray and Chipeta, as they were ordered to do." Slowly and stiffly he got to his feet. He had already been in the saddle far too long. He bowed to Quinket and the White River band. "Again...thank you, my friends."

Josie was saved! Silent tears sprang to my eyes. Why should I weep now? She was saved!

I slept in my own tipi that night, the first time in many nights. It was good to be with Little Bear and Lone Eagle again. Their love was like a warm blanket. I told them a bit about my ride to Mormon Land with Josie's message. And they told me, with great scorn, of Persune's devoted care of Josie.

By the next morning I had made up my mind. I would go to Los Piños Agency with Josie. I would help her and the others along the way if they needed me. I would probably never see her again after she left the Agency. I owed it to her.

I ran to her tipi to tell her. Last night she had been allowed to join her mother in Canalla's tipi. She looked tanned and bright-eyed today. I just then noticed that she had bobbed her blond hair off short. It made her look even younger...and even prettier, I thought.

"I go to Ouray's farm with you!" I announced. "I take care of you on the way!"

"Oh, wonderful!" she laughed. "I'm afraid poor Persune has spoiled me. He always gives me his best pony and his best saddle and his best blankets."

"I can't do that," I laughed with her. "I have only Moonlight."

"And will you kneel down and have me step on your back to mount my pony?" We both giggled.

Arvilla moaned softly in her bed. Poor woman. I couldn't help but feel sorry for her, even though I had never liked her at the Agency. She was too much a part of the despised Father Meeker. But now she looked so frail and shattered with the pain of her hip cruelly printed on her face, my sympathy went out to her in spite of myself.

"I help your mother," I offered. "She needs me."

It was well toward noon by the time we left the Utes behind and set off for Uncompahgre country. The parting was a strange one. Persune was heart-broken. The only bright spot in the horrible massacre, from the Ute point of view, was Persune's newly acquired "bride," as he considered Josie. He had adored her for so long. Now she was his — or had been until Chief Ouray ordered her released to go back to her own people. Persune was weeping openly as she crawled up into the wagon. Josie waved him a carefree goodbye.

Susan, too, was shedding tears. Unable to have any children of her own, she adored Flora Ellen's children. And she had happily accepted the Price woman as just another of Canalla's wives. Her greatest passion was little Johnnie Price. She even begged his mother to sell him to her for three of her best ponies. Flora Ellen just laughed.

But the parting that surprised us all was that of Chief Quinket and Arvilla Meeker. He had treated her so viciously during the first week of her captivity. Even with her wounded hip, he forced her to ride astride a bony-backed pony without a saddle, tossing her about like a bag of rags. But after the night that she had mysteriously cured his little daughter's illness with one of her homeopathic remedies, he was a different Quinket, kindly and considerate, the one we had always known. He now considered her a friend, not one of the hated "whites."

Carefully he lifted her into the high wagon and set her on his own pillow, which he had placed on the wooden seat. He looked up at her for some time, as though groping for the proper words. Finally the words he spoke were a mere whisper. But as I sat on Moonlight close by, I caught every one.

"Thank you, lady," he said softly. "Forgive the Utes for what they have done. And may the Great Sky Father keep you safe!"

"It doesn't matter now," was her quiet response. "I'm an old lady. I'm sixty-four and not long for this world. It's Josie I worry about now."

He took her bony little fingers between his own brown ones and pressed them gently.

"Adios, lady," was his final farewell.
* * * * *

For the next three days I, too, devoted myself to caring for Arvilla. Three horrible days as we rode across the merciless mountains, down off Grand Mesa, across rivers and creeks and canyons, and South, always South, heading for Ouray's farm. But it was for Josie that I did it, not for Mrs. Meeker.

It was late Friday evening before we finally reached Ouray's home. I was surprised to see that it was not a tipi, but a white man's house. It looked just like any of the buildings at White River Agency. I had not expected this.

Chipeta came running out the door as she heard us coming up. Her face was radiating love and kindness. I loved her instantly.

"Oh, my poor dears!" she cried. "Ninety-four miles from your last camp, Ouray says! Ninety-four! You must be miserable! Do come in!" She held out her arms in welcome. She was beautiful still, I decided. Even though no longer the beauty she had been as a girl, she was undeniably beautiful. Maybe it was her beautiful soul shining out.

"I have a hot supper waiting for you. You must be starved!"

She led us into the kitchen, warm with the wonderful fragrance of food. Then she led us on and into the front room, where Chief Ouray sat slumped in a big chair. I could see that he was sick.

Even so, I felt the same warmth and love for him as I felt for Chipeta. He was a great man, and I knew it...as much from my instinct as from all the stories I had heard of him. I felt very small in his company. This was Chief Ouray, our most famous and most powerful of all Ute chieftains. And he had saved Josie!

"Thank God you have all escaped your awful ordeal!" He spoke in a hoarse voice to the group of women and children gathered before him. Little Johnnie was crying quietly on his mother's shoulder while May clung to her mother's skirts in fright. "What next?" was the question in her big blue eyes.

Josie ran impulsively to Ouray and sank to her knees beside him. She took his hand in both hers and kissed it. "Oh, God bless you, sir! You have saved us!"

Arvilla, who limped up to him and bowed her head as low as possible considering her pain-ridden body, followed her. "And may the Lord bless you, sir, and give you peace," she croaked.

Flora Ellen gave him one of her big happy smiles, as she too came forward to shake his hand. "Thanks a million, Chief! We're mighty grateful to ya'!"

And then I knew it was time for me to leave. I had done my best for Josie and her mother. I had delivered them to Chief Ouray, safe and sound. I took Josie's hand and squeezed it, hard.

"Good-bye, dearest friend!" I whispered. Then we fell into each other's arms, both weeping.

"You go home now?" I said, trying to cover my embarrassment.

"Yes. To our big home in Greeley. You come see me there."

"Oh, I will! I will!" I promised.

But that was the last time I was to see my dear Josie, although we little dreamed it then.

Chapter 20

Through the wilderness we rode, Yanko and I. He said he was taking me back to Quinket's camp, but I knew he was eager to get back to the White River Utes to get another glimpse of his beloved.

We did no talking. We just rode and rode and rode. As we had no sleeping equipment, we simply crouched under a tree at night for two or three hours and slept.

The second night we were awakened by an oppressive silence that smothered even the sound of the wind in the pines. It was the soundlessness of snowfall. The mountains lay buried in the first snow of the season. It was not really a snowstorm, for there were no roaring winds, only the soft heavy drifting of snow over the mountains.

Hurriedly we roused ourselves and pushed on for Quinket's camp. We longed to reach the tipis before the snow got too deep. Too cold and exhausted and too numb to be able to think, we finally sighted the lights of campfires in the valley before heavy dark overtook us.

Ah! What a blessing it was to crawl into my familiar bed in Little Bear's tipi and to sink into instant sleep! My blessed grandmother let me sleep all the next day until finally I awoke to a new day, fresh and strong again.

But what of the Utes? This lonely valley high on Grand Mesa was not home. General Adams had ordered us to remain here until the government had decided what to do to us about the Meeker Massacre as the Milk Creek fracas was now called. How long would that be? Who knew? Everyone knew that anything that had to do with the government took forever. Were we doomed to call this isolated spot home? It was so far from the beloved Yampa Valley and from White River, so far from our own Shining Mountains.

The snow had ceased to fall when we saw three bedraggled-looking horsemen come riding in from the West. The alarm went up. Then I recognized Morning Star's buckskin pony. It was indeed Morning Star with two white men. I ran out to meet them.

"Oh, Morning Star!" I cried out. "You're back! You're back! How far did you have to ride?" He looked so weary. I longed to take him in my arms and cradle him.

"I not know. I cannot count the days. But I have help for the captives." He motioned toward his companions. "Good Mormons."

Then I noticed that the two young white men looked nearly as exhausted as Morning Star.

"The white women are free," I told them. "General Adams came and took them to Chief Ouray's home with the Uncompahgre Utes. Then they go back to their own homes."

"Oh, thank God!" exclaimed one.

"Oh, I'm sorry!" said the other. "I'm sorry we couldn't get here any sooner! We wanted to help!"

Quinket then came trudging up through the snow. Morning Star motioned toward his white companions.

"Friend," he said. "Good Mormons."

"I had a message from the captives," I hurried to explain. "I was taking it to get help, but Morning Star took it for me."

Quinket looked from one to another, trying to take it all in, trying to make sense of it. I held my breath. What was he going to do? Would he kill the Mormons? Would he hold them captive for revenge? The silence seemed forever.

At last, without a word, he motioned them to dismount. His face told us nothing. He turned back to the village of tipis, indicating that the Mormons were to follow. We all trooped along. He stopped before his own tipi.

By this time, the entire village had turned out, staring at the newcomers curiously. Quinket's two wives came out the flap of their tipi.

"Food for our guests," he told them. "And after, beds for their rest. They are very tired. Long ride."

Morning Star gave a quick grin of relief. No one had been sure what Quinket would do, especially Morning Star. But he was so weary that he hardly cared. He turned to locate the tipi of his mother, Night Owl.

"Where is Nicaagat's camp?" he asked.

"Just over the hill. On the Eastern slope. Not far," was Quinket's answer.

Morning Star rode off into the night in the direction that the Chief pointed. My heart went with him. I hoped he could find it, in his dazed state.

Next morning early Nicaagat and some of his White River Utes rode over the hill to where our Yampa Utes were camped. At first I was terrified, thinking they had found Morning Star's body, frozen in the snow. I ran out to meet them.

"Did Morning Star find your camp last night?" I called out.

My sense of Ute ways told me that a woman should not be rushing up to a group of men like this and especially not approaching a Ute chieftain so improperly. But I had to know.

Nicaagat nodded. I guess he was accustomed to seeing me always with my father and not with the womenfolk, cooking or tanning deer hides. He didn't seem surprised.

"He is still asleep in his mother's tipi," he said as his group rode past and down to Quinket's tipi.

They dismounted and gathered in a large circle with many of our Yampa Utes. Always curious to know what was going on, I stayed as near the conference as I could without being noticed. They were deeply concerned about preparing for winter. This early snowfall had brought them up short, alerting them to their dangerous predicament. They had no supplies, no permanent winter homes, and no prospect of their abundant White River game for food. Would we starve? Would we perish from the cold? What was going to happen to us, even if we were not pursued by General Merritt's army?

When the council broke up, it was late afternoon. Still nothing had been decided. Nicaagat and his men rode over the hill, leaving us as confused and fearful as before. Would the whites of Colorado wipe us out, as the Governor kept saying? Would Merritt's army ride up here on Grand Mesa and massacre the whole Ute tribe and leave us all lying in pools of frozen blood? I was sick with fear. Was the snow covering my father's body back at Milk Creek?

Three days later an Uncompahgre messenger rode into camp, bringing a copy of a telegram from Washington. Ouray had told him to bring it to me, as I was the only Ute who could read. I was alarmed by his belief in me. True, I could read simple white man's words but not that great spread of new and strange words!

Still I did my best, picking out words I knew and sounding out some of the others. Through great effort and a long time, I managed to give Quinket and Nicaagat an idea of this important message.

It was addressed to General Adams. First it told him how proud President Hayes was of his braveness in putting a stop to the "Ute War," as he called it. Then it said that the Utes were to move to join Chief Ouray's band at Los Piños Agency for now. After a trial, as fair as that for white people, the guilty Utes should be disarmed. The judges for the trial would be Ouray, Adams and someone named Hatch, I think it said.

A large group had gathered around me by the time I had made some sense out of the message. They were as silent as the pine trees as they listened with uncertainty to what I had to say. At last a pent-up breath escaped them.

Nicaagat and Quinket looked at each other and nodded.

"We are safe from the army, then?" asked Quinket.

"Yes, for now anyway."

"And we have to move now to Los Piños Agency? All of us?" asked Nicaagat.

" Now. It says now." He turned to me. "Isn't that what you said?"

I nodded. "Now. All of us."

Our future was frightening to us. It was now winter, and we had to pack up and start moving out into a strange new world we hadn't yet seen. Or rather, the others hadn't seen it. This was so different from our usual winter preparations when we were snug in our own camps, hunting and bringing home game to make into venison jerky and pemmican. We would store the dried food for the Moons-of-Many-Snows when our men could not go out into the woods to hunt.

And when our many people moved in on top of the already full camp of the Uncompahgres, would there be enough game to go around? Of course there wouldn't. Ouray's band would be in trouble as deep as ours. What would we do? Would we all starve? Probably. As we again packed up all our belongings and fastened the tipis and travois to our ponies, our hearts were sick.

But we obeyed the telegram from Washington. Within an hour we had struck camp and were headed South off Grand Mesa. Dark clouds hung low over the mountains ahead of us, warning of more snow to come. Our spirits were as dark and low as the clouds. Because of the massacre, we hadn't received a shipment of supplies for almost two months, and we were destitute. Our children were crying with hunger. There was nothing to give them.

By the fourth day, both camps had arrived at Los Piños Agency. The going had been rough, and Little Bear and Lone Eagle were in great pain with their aching joints and the cold, as were all the Ute elders. I wanted to make them warm and comfortable, but there was no way.

Ouray sent Chipeta out to welcome us with official Uncompahgre greeting and to show us where to pitch our camps. The very warmth of her gracious smile made us feel better. In addition, she told us that we would be served a welcoming feast by the Los Piños Agency. We were soon in high spirits, if even briefly.

By the time we had chosen a spot and each family had pitched its tipi on Uncompahgre land, we could hear a bell ringing at the Agency. It was the call to come for the feast. And a feast it was! Chipeta and other Ute women were dipping up big mugs of hot venison stew and handing out fresh hot chunks of fry bread. Nothing had ever tasted so good. But I couldn't help wondering when the next supply shipment would be coming in for the Agency, according to government contract. I was afraid we were taking the food out of the mouths of our hosts. But no one mentioned it, and I pretended I wasn't worried.

Chapter 21

The following weeks were miserable. On the surface the Uncompahgre Utes welcomed us and treated us well, but underneath we could feel a current of resentment. We were a horde of hungry folk, even though we were friendly Utes who were like a swarm of hungry grasshoppers descending on them. Just by being there, living there, we cut their own food supplies in half.

Now we were all hungry. The game was becoming so scarce that it was almost impossible for the hunters to bring in anything. We even ate beavers and a couple of bears and, as a final indignity, a wolf, which Utes never touched. But it was food. Our children were sick much of the time because of the lack of food. More than one of our White River elders was now bed-ridden because of hunger.

Ouray, may the Great Sky Father bless his noble soul, saved us all more than once that winter, when he allowed us to "hunt" for a "slow elk" as the Uncompahgres called the range cattle, which the government raised for them. Each time we celebrated. And each time we blessed our beloved leader with our prayers.

I thought often of Thunder Cloud, and my heart ached. He had been the center of my life as long as I could remember. But I knew it was for my own loneliness that I wept silently. I was glad for him that he was now in the Land of Forever Summer. There was no hunger there.

We hovered around the Agency, picking up bits of gossip from the outside world and wondering what the Government was planning to do with us. We heard that the captives had been taken from Los Piños, out of the mountains and down into the San Luis Valley, where they were put on a railroad train for Greeley where they had a home. I was relieved at this news.

We also learned that Governor Pitkin had reported to the newspapers that most of Chief Ouray's warriors had taken an active part in the battle against Thornburgh at Milk Creek. We were furious at this open lie, but what could we do? Pitkin was using everything possible in his campaign, "The Utes must go!" He wanted to exterminate every Ute in the state so that the swarms of white settlers waiting for word of free land could come pouring in.

But I think that the one thing that hurt us most of all was the loss of our ponies. All we had were the few we rode and the few extras we used to pull our travois. The rest we had abandoned to the wild at White River. Where were they now? Where was my own Snowball? Now a full-grown horse, a beautiful yearling, he had followed me around a good deal and loved being petted and having his black velvet nose stroked. I should be there now, strapping a blanket to his back and breaking him to ride. Where was he? How was he doing? How would he survive the coming winter? And all the great herd of Thunder Cloud's ponies? Who owned them now? Who was taking care of them?

Then the gossip from the outside began to turn to the "outrages" performed upon the captives during their twenty-six days in the custody of the Utes. Our good friend, General Adams, had gone on to Greeley to have personal interviews with each woman to see if they had been forcibly raped. Of course they had, as we all knew. It was the Ute way of vengeance and a part of our rules of warfare.

I thought of each woman and how she had been treated within my own sight. Each one was such a different story. I was sure Persune had not "raped" Josie. He had adored her and had openly courted her for so long. That had been his only reason for going to school, day after day. He had hoped he could win her in the usual Ute way, by mutual consent to marriage. He honored her.

After the massacre, he had taken her as his "wife" to protect her from any attack from war-fired warriors. He had cherished her, spoiled her, and showered her with his attentions, day and night. I had no doubt that they had shared the same marriage bed for twenty-six nights, but as for physical attacks, I felt sure that had never happened. He thought he had her as his wife until she was taken away from him.

Quinket, I had no doubt, had avenged himself upon Arvilla Meeker the night of the massacre. I recalled that night vividly. The moon was shining, and I remembered him in the unprecedented act of drinking himself into a state of violence. I recalled both the bottle of liquor he kept swigging from and his frequently tipping up the bottle in the moonlight to measure its contents.

Then I recalled the night of his little girl's illness and Arvilla's curing potion. From that night onward, Quinket ceased tossing her around like a bag of potatoes and began treating her with the gentlest solicitude. Again he was the Quinket I had always known.

As for Flora Ellen, she was a story of her own. Voluptuous and as innocent as a child, she had been eyed by every man at White River, I suppose. But I think that her being taken as our Medicine Man's captive is what saved her life. I think he took her for that very reason. He took proper Ute vengeance, but in so doing, he had protected her and her children from the violence of the young warriors for the rest of their captivity.

War is war. I remembered hearing the stories of other Indian tribes on the Plains and of their unfair treatment by the whites avenging themselves for native violence. Unlike the farm wife in Kansas who had been nailed alive to her cabin door or the Nebraska bride who had been roasted alive in a slow fire, the White River captives were lucky.

The Ute Peace Commission, which met for two long and boring months from mid-November until well into January, was held in a ramshackle cottonwood barn at Los Piños. The three commissioners who were to decide the fate of the Utes were General Adams, Chief Ouray, and General Hatch, a stranger to us.

None of us were ever allowed in to the hearings, but there was a large group of whites, newspaper reporters and such like, who hung around the door, hoping to overhear any news possible from the secret meetings.

Many of the meetings had to be cancelled because of Ouray's growing illness. He was dying of a disease that his white doctors called Bright's Disease, but he was determined to hang on until he had saved his beloved Utes. He could see the final curtain falling on his own life at the same time that it was falling on the lives of his people. It was a terrible time for all of us.

On the days when he was barely able to get out of bed at his farm, he would be taken in his big Germantown carriage to the barn, where he took his place at the hearing table. But his mind was as sharp as ever. It was only his body that was failing him at the youthful age of forty-six.

We hung around as near the hearings as we could. But Ouray had assigned a large Ute police force to guard the hearings. He knew his own life was in danger of assassination if some of the hotheaded young warriors should overhear something that would set them off. And so we really couldn't get all that was going on.

We knew that the Commission's biggest problem was to persuade the Utes, after the guilt of the crimes was decided, to combine with the Uintah Utes of Utah, the Uncompahgre Utes, and the White River Utes to form a group to agree to give up their ten-million-acre Reservation in return for payment of past money due them on old treaties. It wasn't going to be easy.

One reason that the hearings took so long was that Ouray was the only one who could understand both English and Ute. He had to translate everything that was said so that everyone knew what was going on. Both General Adams and Chief Ouray took courage by the knowledge that as the hearing dragged on, war was growing less likely. The mountain passes were piling deep with snow and any military maneuvers by either side were now becoming almost impossible.

We heard that as each Ute gave his testimony about what actually happened at White River and Milk Creek, each story was as different as night and day. No sense could be made to any of it. The judges were in a quandary as to what had really taken place. And General Hatch demanded that the women be brought back to Los Piños to give their testimony in person.

Both Ouray and Adams quickly squashed this plan. They already had all their interviews in written form, and these two did not want the poor women to have to be dragged back into the mountains for such an ordeal.

Finally the decision was made and a list of twelve Utes who had to stand trial was made. At the top, of course, were Quinket, Canalla, and Persune. The others were only afterthoughts, we decided. Adams declared that the Milk Creek battle was an unavoidable mistake on both sides, and so no guilt was decided on that score. It was decided that the twelve on the list should be sent by train to the Government prison in Leavenworth until the trial, and that the trial would take place outside Colorado. This was the final decision, sent by telegraph from Washington from the head of Indian Affairs there.

We shuddered in the cold as General Adams gave us his report. It was over. For now, at least. With drooping heads we went back to our icy tipis. Where to next? Would I ever again see my Yampa valley? Or my Shining Mountains? Or Snowball?

Chapter 22

In the bitter cold of the new Moon, we gathered at Los Piños Agency to see our Ute delegation set off for Washington. Ouray was far too sick to go, but bolstered by his grim determination to take care of his people as long as there was a faint hint of life left in his failing body, he was determined to go so he was here with the others.

It was early morning with the sun barely touching the tips of the Uncompahgre peaks and the valley still frozen in shadows when they loaded up for departure, headed for the train at Alamosa. Ouray was accompanied on one side by Shavano and on the other by Nicaagat. With great reverence they followed him to his carriage and tucked him inside, wrapping him warmly in a heavy buffalo robe.

Behind him came Chipeta, radiant in her beautiful white doeskin dress that she always wore to Washington. At the Agency office, we had seen pictures of her taken in Washington and calling her "Queen Chipeta." She and Ouray were now front-page news, as the Meeker Massacre had brought the attention of the whole country upon the Utes. Most of the stories in the papers were lies, of course, but Ute stories sold lots of papers.

We all pressed close, softly calling out our prayers and blessings to our great leader. What he would accomplish in Washington was a mystery to us, but we believed in him and repeated our most deep-felt prayers for his mission. And with genuine love, we all said good-bye to Chipeta as well. Tears were hot on my cheeks.

As they drove off into the lightening dawn, we stood hushed. A warm hand crept over my icy one and pressed it gently. It was Morning Star. In the hubbub of the past weeks of nightmare, we had scarcely seen each other. And when we had, we were so numb with torment that we scarcely recognized one another.

"May the Great White Father in Washington treat them well," he said. And it was like a prayer. I think it was, whispered close to my ear. This moment was bigger than us, bigger than our love for one another. It was the very lives of our people we were praying for.

"And may the Great Sky Father of us all care for them on this dangerous journey," I whispered back, pressing his hand. Mine was beginning to warm in his clasp. I brushed my tears aside, and then I was with Little Bear and Lone Eagle again and Morning Star was lost in the silent crowd.

We learned much later that Ouray was able to sign a most remarkable treaty, the wisest and fairest of any treaty ever signed with an Indian tribe, either before or since. Ouray knew that the Utes had to learn to live with the whites, difficult as it was. And this treaty arranged for that.

Every Ute was to receive 160 acres of land as his own, a "farm" to do with as he would on his own reservation. And the Ute land outside the Reservation was to be sold to whites, with the proceeds to be paid to the Utes.

Ouray's treaty also agreed to pay the survivors of the victims at the White River Agency a specified amount each, an amount considered fair by the Secretary of Indian Affairs, by Congress, and by the Ute delegation.

But the most delicate issue of all, that of the "punishment" of the Utes for the Meeker Massacre, was the hardest for all to agree on. They studied over the list of twelve, which had been prepared by the three-man Commission in the cottonwood barn the month before. They finally settled on three Utes to be sent to trial at the Government prison at Leavenworth. The "guilty" were Quinket, Tim Johnson, who was the teenaged son of Canalla, and a Uintah Ute, who "just happened to be at White River" the day of the Massacre.

We had no idea why Quinket was singled out as one of the culprits. But it was easy to figure out why the Uintah Ute was named. He was a stranger, and they probably figured that he was up to mischief for the Mormons in some way. As for Tim Johnson, he was one of the hotheaded young fellows who had shot at Shadrach Price when he began plowing up the racetrack. And besides, Flora Ellen had told Adams that he had bragged of killing William Post.

We were all surprised one evening a month later to see General Adams and Nicaagat ride up to the Los Piños Agency. They had come all the way from Washington to pick up Quinket, Tim Johnson, and the Uintah Ute who, we knew now, was with us to court a White River girl.

When the Utah Uintah Ute was informed of his destination, he swore that he would stand trial in Washington and nowhere else. The next morning he was gone. We never saw him again, but we rejoiced over his escape for we knew that he was innocent.

The White River Ute tipis were pitched the entire nine-mile distance along the road from Ouray and Chipeta's farm down to the Los Piños Agency. It became a kind of Ute telegraph system in itself as word was passed along from one tipi to the next. Little Bear's tipi, my home, was one of those nearest the Agency, so we were near the source of all news coming out of Washington. We felt fortunate, as we were not sure how much of that news was misquoted as it passed along the Ute telegraph. The new Agent was good about releasing Washington news to us as soon as he heard it.

I didn't need the telegraph system to know what went on that icy evening when General Adams and Nicaagat came to pick up the two Utes to be delivered to Fort Leavenworth. All the Utes in the vicinity crowded around Chief "Jack," as Nicaagat was known by the whites, to find out what was going on. Our lives depended upon it.

"Be ready by sunrise in the morning to go to Leavenworth with us," Nicaagat told the two "guilty" Utes, as we all gathered before the Agency office. The sky behind the buildings was turning from pale rose to green to black as night crept up on us.

"The earlier we start, the better it will be," added our good friend, General Adams. "As soon as we leave you at Leavenworth, we have to hurry back to Washington. We must be there to protect the rights of the Utes during these hearings."

My heart ached for Tim Johnson, our Medicine Man's young son, who was sobbing openly on Canalla's shoulder.

"Will they kill me, Father?" he blubbered. He clung to his father like a little, lost child. He was sixteen years old, only a child, although his large size made him look older. He was as tall as Canalla, and he looked a little foolish now.

"Be brave, my son," Canalla pressed him tight in his arms. "Be a man."

But Tim was frightened, too frightened for his brief years to handle. He was not to be comforted. Susan looped her arm through his and led him back to their tipi nearby. She was Ouray's sister, and one of Canalla's wives, so Tim was one of her own family.

With Tim's departure, our group seemed suddenly very still. Quinket stood in the center of the great circle of friends. He too was silent and kicked at the frozen snow with his moccasined foot.

"I can't tell you how sorry I am about this," the General said, his hand on Quinket's shoulder. And he truly was, for he had been a good friend of the Utes, and especially this Yampa Ute chieftain who had in turn been a loyal friend of the whites, for many years.

"I am deeply sorry," he repeated. "I tried to talk them out of this, but I have failed." There was no smile now on his wide Dutch face, only a sorrow as deep as Quinket's.

Then, suddenly, the old chief stood up as tall as he could and looked around him, straight into the faces of his friends.

"I say here," he spoke out clear and distinct in the night air, "I was at White River Agency that bad day when white men were killed. But I was in the storeroom, counting our bags of flour. I no see who did shooting. I not know who did it. It was a terrible bad mistake. But I go to Leavenworth. I will not fight it. I will be the ...What do you say? The goat? I will be the goat, so the White Father in Washington will leave my people in peace. I go now."

He turned and walked off to his own tipi. Good brave Quinket. I was so proud at that moment that he was our Yampa Ute Chief. And I couldn't help looking at Nicaagat, the White River Chief, who had so often been the angry rival of Quinket in the old days. Now he was Quinket's jailer, the man who was taking him to Leavenworth. It didn't seem fair. But life, I decided at that moment, is never fair.

Poor Tim Johnson was still sobbing the next morning as Adams and Nicaagat departed with their two prisoners for Leavenworth. He was terrified, we all knew. It wasn't until much later that we learned that he had cried all the way to the Kansas prison, where they were to leave him and Quinket. But he continued to weep so hysterically; they didn't have the heart to leave him. Instead they took him on to Washington with them, where he stayed in the Hotel Tremont during the rest of the hearing, sitting in isolation in his room.

Then we heard that Josie had gone to Washington to testify. The reporters were charmed with her usual laughter and beauty. She was not really beautiful, but she had a sort of magic that made everyone feel that she was. Her testimony did nothing to harm the Utes and, instead, delighted Mr. Schurz, the head of Indian Affairs in Washington. And it made a good newspaper story. The hearings were closed to the press, but reporters kept their sharp eyes open for a good story, and Josie made a good one.

Another witness who did the Utes proud was "Queen" Chipeta. She honestly declared she knew nothing of the Massacre, of Meeker, or of the events of White River. The Committee released her interview to the newspapers, but the story that took front-page news was probably all lies, made up by some reporter with a good imagination.

"When she took the stand on March 19," he wrote, "Queen Chipeta was tastefully arrayed in a seal-skin saque, silk dress and fashionable hat." From this, we knew that he had never seen Chipeta.

The poor Utes who were on the Committee were "entertained" to boredom. The various "hosts" who rolled out the red carpet for them must have gotten their cues mixed, for they were taken to Mount Vernon four times. Their other expeditions were just as boring and repetitious. After a time, the Utes would go to sleep as soon as they were put in a sightseeing carriage. Washington became an endurance test for them.

Colorado's Senator Teller giving a long, long speech, which rewrote history and put the rest of the senators to sleep, finally ended the hearing. He pointed out how the Utes had always harassed the whites and had killed countless Colorado taxpayers. All lies, of course. No Ute had ever killed a Colorado taxpayer.

After four long months of this, Chief Ouray, "Queen" Chipeta, and the Ute delegation returned to Los Piños. We turned out in joy to see them home. And still Ouray lived, proud that he had saved his people from Teller's demand for Ute extinction. We heard from the singing wire in Lake City that the Senate had passed the Ute Bill 1509 with flying colors. What Ouray had demanded, he got. But what was it?

We were not to learn until months later. The Southern Utes had to sign it first. And Chief Ouray was not sure that they would. They had not had a part in the Commission's work and knew nothing of it.

Chapter 23

Senator Teller had announced to the world that Colorado would be open for white settlement the moment Senate Bill 1509 was passed. And so, long before the bill passed, thousands of land-hungry whites headed for Los Piños. For miles up from the San Luis Valley, the road was crowded with wagons, pack trains, carriages, gamblers, bartenders, miners, and farmers. Thousands of them and they kept coming! They all wanted Ute land.

When he heard our cry for help from our own Agent, Secretary Schurz sent in an army of six hundred soldiers. Many whites thought the soldiers were there to protect them from the raging Utes. True, we were raging inside but, in reality, we were cowering in our tipis, waiting to see what horror would attack us next.

Schurz, in Washington, had a deep heart of sympathy for the Utes and worked with Chief Ouray in every way he could to help us. But when this huge army, six hundred of them, marched into the middle of us and planted their headquarters in the exact center of the White River Utes, halfway between Ouray's farm and the Los Piños Agency, we were terrified, in spite of Ouray's promises.

Poor Ouray, sick as he was, kept trying to explain to us that Secretary Schurz had sent the soldiers to protect us, not the whites. But from past experience with the Government, it was hard to convince us. How could he reassure us that we were being crowded off the Earth, our own beloved Earth, for our own good? It was impossible.

As we watched the soldiers patrolling the borders of the Reservation and booting the greedy whites off Indian land as soon as they would sneak across, we realized that Ouray was right. They were trying to protect us. Even with protection from the soldiers, we hung around the Agency and our tipis, waiting in fear for whatever was going to happen next. We were mostly silent and terrified, our young braves ready to explode at any moment. They felt that their days on this Earth were limited. Governor Pitkin kept repeating, "The Utes must go!" And we believed it.

Even the high Uncompahgre Mountains around the North Fork of the Gunnison were baking in the July heat when the five-man Ute Commission arrived at the Agency to get the "yes" vote from the Utes on the new law. Ouray realized that he was nearing the end. He asked Sapovanero to take his place in getting the Ute males to touch the clerk's pen. That was the sign that they had agreed to the treaty. Thus the Ute bill was "signed" by almost all the White River and Uncompahgre men.

But before the long and tedious "signing" was complete, some of the Utes boiled over. The treaty said that the White River Utes were to be settled on the land around the junction of the Grand and Gunnison Rivers. This wouldn't have upset our tribe too much. We would still be close to our old hunting grounds. Close enough for the fall hunt, anyway.

Then the Commission discovered that there wasn't enough land in the area for each Ute's 160-acre parcel. So they decided to send us to Utah with Ouray's people, to be joined up with the Uintah Utes. That idea was what sparked fire. It infuriated us.

Many of the Uncompahgre Utes were already packed up and started on their 350-mile journey to Utah when the shooting started. General Mackenzie had set his cavalry, infantry, artillery and signalmen on the mesa above the river to guard the Utes as they departed for their new Reservation in the far West. Suddenly Mackenzie saw unusual movement in the valley below. He quickly peered through his field glasses. There, coming toward him at full gallop, was the huge-bellied Colorow. Stunned, we watched the show from the valley. He was followed by fifty of our young warriors, bright in war paint and eagle feathers. Well-armed, they began shooting. It was a furious attack, a last-ditch stand.

Then all hell broke loose. Mackenzie gave the signal, and the whole mesa seemed to explode. Thunder, lightning, smoke and earthquake roared from the guns above. It didn't take Colorow long to see his mistake. Although he and his followers had pledged to fight the whites "to the death," he seemed to decide it wasn't worth it. He had become famous in the early days of Colorado Territory as the "Biscuit-Eater," harassing every pioneer wife in the area, entering kitchens uninvited and begging for biscuits. Now his shaggy head sank to his chest. He turned and led his band back into the valley. It was a brave but futile exhibition. We admired his courage but knew it was useless. We were doomed.

It was the Moon-of-Ripening-Cherries, August, before the Commission was through with us at Los Piños, and we headed out for the Southern Ute Reservation at Ignacio. Chief Ouray knew he shouldn't attempt the trip. The doctor warned him that his Bright's disease was bad. Still Ouray worried about us.

He was afraid that Chief Ignacio and Buckskin Charlie of the Southern Utes wouldn't sign the treaty. They had lived too far away to know what was going on. What if they refused? They too were a big part of the Utes of Colorado. That could be enough to cause a Ute war!

Ouray ordered Sapovanero to get him his horse, for he was too tired to walk, let alone ride. With stubborn determination, he set off for Ignacio, one hundred and thirty miles to the South, through rugged wilderness and rough mountains. With him went his white doctor, Chipeta and her brother, John McCook, and a few friends.

It was August 15 when we all gathered at Los Piños to see him off. Again Morning Star was at my elbow.

"He has big courage," he said quietly.

"Yes," I whispered. "We will never see him again." Again my hand was in Morning Star's hand. He pressed my fingers so hard it hurt. I knew he agreed.

"And may the Great Sky Father help him in his final task," I prayed aloud.

Wordless, Ouray clung to his pony, as they struggled, stumbled, slid, leaped and staggered through canyons, gulches and over towering mountain passes. It would be the last time he would ever see his beautiful Shining Mountains, the last time he would see the high mountain meadows blazing with the scarlet of Indian paint brush, as the whites called the native flower, and the last time he would see the columbines.

Later we learned that Ouray and his little party had taken a shortcut through the mountains so they could arrive at Ignacio before the lumbering wagon of the Ute Commission. He reached there on August 17. Totally exhausted, he slept for two days.

But when the Ute Commission opened their hearings on August 20, Chief Ouray was sitting at the table, as sharp and alert as ever. For the next two days, he talked with the Southern Ute leaders, explaining the whole thing to them and convincing them how important it was to them to sign the treaty. They promised.

The next day, August 24, 1880, at 11 A.M. he breathed his last.

Chipeta and his friends wrapped him in a blanket and buried him, with a few dead ponies, under a huge rock in a secret little canyon near Ignacio.

Chief Ouray, the greatest Ute who ever lived, was gone. Now poor Chipeta was alone. And we were, too.

Chapter 24

Then one brilliant golden day in mid-September, someone came to our tipi with an urgent message for me to come to the Los Piños Agency as soon as possible. I was terrified. What in the world had I done? I dropped the comb with which I was combing Little Bear's hair and flew to the Agency as fast as my moccasins would fly.

"You have a letter," the Agent announced the minute that I got there. His tone was like a dark warning. I could see he was greatly disturbed.

"Me? A letter?" I couldn't have been more surprised if he had said the Great White Father in Washington had sent for me. A letter? I knew what a letter was from the days in the Agent's office, back at White River. But no one I ever knew, except the whites, had ever received one.

"Were you expecting one?" he asked, his eyes drilling into mine. It was like he was accusing me of something bad.

"No! Who would I get a letter from?"

He looked at the small white letter in his hands as though he had the evidence of my crime.

"It says here," and he carefully read the upper corner of the envelope, "From Miss Josephine Meeker."

"Josie!" I almost shouted. "How could she find me?"

"It wasn't easy, apparently," the Agent said, with a hint of a smile. "From the looks of this envelope, it's done a lot of traveling. One address after another has been crossed out."

I reached out my hand for it. But still he held it.

"You are Mollie Flying Horse, aren't you? Of the Yampa Utes?"

I still held out my hand. It was my letter, wasn't it?

"Yes." A letter from Josie! And he wouldn't let me have it!

"Can you read?" He drilled me again with his cold hard eyes.

"Yes. A little," I admitted.

Slowly he handed it to me, as though he wasn't sure it was the right thing to do. I stared at the precious letter. A letter from my dear

Josie! I recognized her handwriting and my name, Flying Horse Mollie. I had learned to write that much in school. That was the only thing I could write, but I could read a little more than that if I worked at it and sounded out every word.

Carefully I opened the letter. It even smelled like Josie! Struggling, I sounded out the message, word by word.

My dear Mollie:

How are you, little friend? I pray you are well. I hear that the Utes are soon going to Utah to a new Reservation. I hope you will be safe and happy there.

I am now living in Washington and have a good job with the Department that takes care of Indian Affairs. I am an assistant private secretary to Senator Teller from Colorado. I live here alone at a boarding house with other people, none of my own family.

My mother lives alone in Greeley, with a house full of chickens, ducks and turkeys, she says. (It sounds awful, doesn't it?)

My brother Ralph lives in New York, where he is a writer for the big newspapers there, like my father used to be. He comes to Washington to see me once in a while. He just got married and is very happy.

I am very happy, too, and hope you are.

> *With much love,*
> *Josie*

My dear, beloved Josie! What a beautiful, miraculous thing a letter was! It was almost like talking with her! A letter! I slipped it back into its envelope and pressed it to my heart. I would treasure it forever!

Finally I came to my senses in the real world. I was still standing in the Agent's office where I was standing when he handed me the letter. He stared at me like I was crazy, for I knew that I was smiling like a silly goose. I was so happy at that moment, I could have laughed out loud. I turned and ran from the Agency and back to our tipi. I would read the letter to Little Bear. A letter!

* * * * *

The Agent had warned us that our band was to be next in line to set out for the Uintah Reservation somewhere near the edge of the world, it seemed. What it would be like, only our nightmares told us. We had already been issued our travel provisions, a meager supply, which we doubted would last us those long, long days of dragging through the wilderness.

I had already been part of the way into Utah when I was carrying Josie's note to the Uintahs for help. As I remembered it in my tumbled memory, it was a desolate, ugly place. We all shivered with the announcement of our departure.

It was already late November, and snow was deep on our Shining Mountains. The next morning at sun-up, we were to strike our tipis and set off for the end of the world. I found it very hard to go to sleep. My bones already ached with the cold.

But I dreamed I heard a flute. It was a beautiful sound. On and on it played, and I was soothed by the gentle melody. I slept, soundly it seemed, for a long while. But gradually I was pulled out of my deep sleep by the persistent music of the flute. I woke fully. It was not a dream. It was real!

I crawled out of my buffalo robes, softly, so as not to awaken my grandparents. But Lone Eagle spoke out in the darkness. His voice sounded a little grumpy, as grumpy as he ever got with me.

"I wondered if you would ever hear it."

"I was asleep," I whispered. "Who in the world...?"

"You do not know?"

"No! I have never heard that beautiful music before. Have you?"

I thought he laughed. But I couldn't understand why. "No," was his only answer.

I slipped into my moccasins and opened the flaps of our tipi. There stood Morning Star with a flute to his lips. Dawn was just beginning to paint the eastern sky with wild rose pink. He lowered the flute, his dark, shining eyes wide with questions.

Then I remembered! Little Bear had told me the legend of long ago when I was a child. A flute playing in a young woman's dreams was an invitation to marriage!

I opened my arms to him. Dear, beautiful Morning Star! His arms went around me, warm and tight.

"Come in! Come in!" I whispered, pulling back the flaps of the tipi. But there was no need to whisper now. Both Lone Eagle and Little Bear were up.

"Welcome!" said Little Bear. There was a happy smile on her face, the first smile I had seen there for ages, it seemed. Indeed, as we had recently so little to smile about, no one had smiled. "Welcome to our family!"

"Welcome! Welcome!" echoed Lone Eagle. He too opened his arms and pressed Morning Star to him.

Then Morning Star turned to me and took me in his arms. His kiss was hard and warm against my lips. I was his — forever.

*****

We were two days on the desolate trail. To be driven off the face of the Earth was still more than we could understand! Even though Chief Ouray had spent so much time and love trying to help us understand, it was more than we could grasp.

Just after we had paused for a noon rest break, a runner from the Agency overtook us.

"Mollie! Mollie Flying Horse!" he gasped, trying to call out as he ran.

I hadn't heard him at first, until others repeated the call. I was too frightened to answer even when I heard my name. My heart seemed to freeze. Something terrible had happened, I knew, but what? What could be worse than what were enduring?

"Here she is!" someone shouted.

The Uncompahgre runner came up to me just as I slipped from Moonlight's back to stand beside her.

"Here," were his hoarse words. "A letter! The Agent said to get it to you before you got away."

Another letter? Another letter from Josie? The sun suddenly seemed to shine out through the snow.

I took it quickly and looked at it. My heart sank. It was not in Josie's familiar handwriting. It was typed. My fingers shook as I opened it. I read:

Dear Mollie,

I am Ralph Meeker, Josie's brother. I know you were a good friend of hers so I am writing to you. I found her ill when I visited her in Washington last week. She had just missed two days work with a bad cold. I called a doctor, who said it was pneumonia. She was dead two hours later. I am sorry to tell you this. My best wishes for you there.

Sincerely,

Ralph Meeker

Dear, dear Josie! A million years I stood there, my face pressed against Moonlight's neck. I was numb. I could no longer think. The world was dead. There was no future, no past — nothing, nothing but an empty heart. I couldn't even cry. There were no tears. Only the terrible aching emptiness.

And then, after an endless time, time that went on and on and on without changing anything, I found myself in the warm comforting arms of my husband.

Morning Star lifted my chin to look into my face. And then the tears broke loose. My face was swimming in spring rain. He kissed my lips, gently.

"It's Josie," I whispered. "She...she's...dead."

The words seemed to drop from my tongue like rocks. They were such ugly words! Morning Star's arms seemed to rock me a little. And I was comforted, like when Little Bear used to rock me as a child.

"She is safe then. Safe forever with our Great Father in the Sky," he whispered against my hair.

And I felt safe, too. No matter what lay ahead, I would be safe, as long as Morning Star was near. Dear, dear Morning Star!

Suddenly I felt a strange movement under my heart. It was real. Or had I imagined it? There it was, moving again! It was real! Was my heart telling me something? I put Morning Star's hand gently over the soft movement.

"Can you feel it?" I whispered.

His hand rested there tenderly a long moment. There it was again!

He bent and kissed me, ever so gently, again and again. Then he stood tall and pressed me in his arms.

"Yes!' he whispered, and his voice was shaking with excitement. I had never heard him like this before. "It is our child! Our new and shining child!" I felt his heart thumping hard against mine, and my heart raced in answer.

"Our child!" he said aloud. "We must hurry! We will carry it to our new land to be born!"

And so, with the winter blizzard howling around our ears, we climbed on our ponies and set out for the blinding West that was Utah, our new land.

Never again might we see our beautiful Shining Mountains, but we would see our beautiful new and shining child! And we would be together! We must hurry!

My heart was singing. Our child was a sacred spirit fresh from the spirit world and we would cherish her. And we would name her Hope. In the frozen deserts of Utah she would be our blessing from the Great Spirit.

BIBLIOGRAPHY

Bierhorst, John - *In The Trail of the Wind: American Indian Poems and Ritual Orations*, New York, Farraf, Straus and Giroux, 1971.

Brown, Dee - *Bury My Heart at Wounded Knee: An Indian History of the American West*, New York, Holt, Rinehart and Winston, 1971

Carter, Forrest - *The Education of Little Tree*, Albuquerque, University of New Mexico Press, 1997

Castro, Michael - *Interpreting the Indian: Twentieth Century Poets and the Native American*, Norman and London, University of Oklahoma Press, 1991.

Clark, Ella E. - *Indian Legends from the Northern Rockies*, Norman and London, University of Oklahoma Press, 1988.

Cronyn, George W. - *American Indian Poetry: An Anthology of Songs and Chants*, New York, Liveright, 1934.

Crum, Sally - *People of the Red Earth: American Indians of Colorado*, Santa Fe, Ancient City Press, 1996.

Culin, Stewart - *Games of the North American Indian: Volume 1, Games of Chance*, Lincoln and London, University of Nebraska Press, 1992.

Culin, Stewart - *Games of the North American Indian: Volume 2, Games of Skill*, Lincoln and London, University of Nebraska Press, 1992.

Culin, Stewart - *O Brave New Words: Native American Loanwords in Current English*, Lincoln and London, University of Nebraska Press, 1992.

Day, A. Grove - *The Sky Clears: Poetry of the American Indians*, Lincoln and London, University of Nebraska Press, 1964.

Hausman, Gerald -*Turtle Island Alphabet: A Lexicon of Native American Symbols and Culture*, New York, St. Martin's Press, 1992.

Hebard, Grace Raymond - *Washakie: Chief of the Shoshones*, Lincoln and London, University of Nebraska Press, 1995.

Larson, Robert W. - *Red Cloud: Warrior-Statesman of the Lakota Sioux*, Norman and London, University of Oklahoma Press, 1997.

Lawson, Michael - *Damned Indians: The Pick-Sloan Plan and the Missouri River Sioux, 1944-1980,* Norman and London, University of Oklahoma Press, 1982.

Margolin, Malcolm - *Native Ways: California Indian Stories and Memories,* Berkeley, Heyday Books, 1995.

Margolin, Malcolm - *The Way We Lived: California Indian Reminiscences, Stories and Songs,* Berkeley, Heyday Books, 1981.

Marsh, Charles S. - *People of the Shining Mountains: The Utes of Colorado,* Boulder, Pruett Publishing Company, 1982.

Merton, Thomas - *Ishi Means Man,* Greensboro, Unicorn Press, 1976.

Mourning Dove - *A Salishan Autobiography,* Lincoln and London, University of Nebraska Press, 1990.

Neihardt, John G. - *Black Elk Speaks: The Legendary "Book of Visions" of an American Indian,* Lincoln and London, University of Nebraska Press, 1972.

Pettit, Jan - *Utes: The Mountain People,* Boulder, Johnson Books, 1990.

Rosen, Kenneth - *The Man Who Sends Rain Clouds: Contemporary Stories by American Indians,* New York, Random House Inc., 1975.

Sprague, Marshall - *Massacre: The Tragedy at White River,* Lincoln and London, University of Nebraska Press, 1957.

Thompson, Lucy - *Reminiscences of a Yurok Woman,* Berkeley, Heyday Books, 1991.
Walking Turtle, Eagle, Indian America: A Traveler's Companion, Santa Fe, John Muir Publications, 1995.

Wallis, Velma - *Two Old Women: An Alaskan Legend of Betrayal, Courage and Survival,* New York, Harper Collins Publishers Inc., 1993.

Wilson, Gilbert L. - *Waheenee: An Indian Girl's Story,* Lincoln and London, University of Nebraska Press, 1981.

Wissler, Clark - *Indians of the United States,* New York, Doubleday, 1966.

Young, Richard K. - *The Ute Indians of Colorado in the Twentieth Century,* Norman and London, University of Oklahoma Press, 1997.